LOU TULLIO:
A REAL ERIE GUY

A revealing look at the life and times of one of
the most significant and heavily mythologized
politicians in the history of Erie, Pennsylvania

Cory Vaillancourt

A Jefferson Educational Society Publication
Erie, Pennsylvania

WRECKED ANGLE

Library of Congress Card Number: 2015948931
ISBN: 978-0-692-50736-0

Printed in the United States of America by
Gohrs Printing Service, a division of Haines Printing.

Book layout and design by Todd Scalise and Kayla Nesselhauf of
Higherglyphics LLC.

First Jefferson Educational Society Mass Market Edition:
October 2015

for my dad, who taught me to love reading
for my mom, who taught me to love writing
for my daughter, who taught me to love

FORWARD

In September 2014 – well in advance of the 50th anniversary of Lou Tullio's first electoral victory – I was honored to be commissioned by the Jefferson Educational Society (Erie's think tank for community progress) to craft the most substantive and authoritative work ever written about this legendary former Erie mayor; it took longer – and was longer – than any of us expected, but the most important figure in Erie's history since Commodore Oliver Hazard Perry and until Governor (and later, the first Secretary of United States Department of Homeland Security) Tom Ridge deserved no less a treatment. And we all know that opening a bottle of wine before it is truly ready only leads to sour grapes.

This work, however, is not a standalone entity; it was built atop the visionary work of many craftsmen before me.

In 1973, Jefferson Educational Society President Dr. William P. Garvey submitted his doctoral dissertation to the University of Pittsburgh. Titled "The Ethnic Factor in Erie Politics" it both postulated and to a great extent proved how election results in Erie were (and are) the result of decades-long ethnopolitical trends. Garvey's dissertation – influenced by the work of Yale Sociologist J. K. Myers and bolstered by local electoral data Garvey himself methodically collected – makes him, truly, the architect of this work.

If Garvey was the draftsman, Erie County Councilman Dr. Kyle Foust dug the foundation. His comprehensive work, "Why Lou Tullio: How Erie's Most Powerful Mayor Came to Power" appeared in the Journal of Erie Studies in 2003 but had first emerged as a product of his academic career years earlier. Foust delivered on his ambitious title – his assessment of the period just before Tullio hit the Fifth Floor of City Hall is the groundwork that underlies this assemblage.

If Foust dug the foundation, Jefferson Educational Society Vice President and Executive Director Ferki Ferati fashioned the infrastructure – the steely bones that would provide support and substance.

In the Louis J. Tullio Collection of the Sister Mary Franklin Lawrence Archival Center in the basement of the Hamermill Library at Mercyhurst University in Erie, Pennsylvania lie 49 different scrapbooks – two feet by two feet in size – in which reside a meticulously curated collection of almost every imaginable scrap of print published about Lou Tullio during his time as Mayor of the City of Erie.

Ferati combed through every one of them, recording the dates and the headlines and the publications, summarizing the contents of each article – often quoting at length – and putting all of that into a fully searchable digital file. Newspaper articles, from the 1960s – digitized to be fully searchable. It's amazing, isn't it? Ferati's work totaled 175,655 words.

All searchable.

In English.

Which is neither his first nor second language.

So if I wanted to search for "Paxton" or "Nixon" or "Bolo" or "Bags" or even "19th street," I could.

Garvey's foresight, Foust's foundation, and Ferati's framework allowed me to erect this skyscraper, which in reality consists of dozens upon dozens of stories – Lou Tullio: A Real Erie Guy incorporates more than 500 citations, includes hundreds of print sources, and utilizes 40-odd hours of audio interviews with more than a dozen of Tullio's contemporaries that resulted in a master transcript exceeding 65,000 words; paring all that down to just 40,000 words covering several centuries of Erie's political geography took eight months, and then another three months to edit.

And then, after sorting through hundreds of photographs and spending another month on layout and design, it was done.

But it's not done. Not really. Nothing ever really is; historians, it is said, are able to see so far only because they stand on the shoulders of giants.

Accordingly, my greatest hope for this work is not that it inform those who lived it; my greatest hope is not that it educate those who lead us; my greatest hope is not that it illuminate those dark corners of the sausage factory where the gears of government grind.

Those are indeed hopes – but my greatest hope is that this thing that I've built in conjunction with the architect and the excavator and the steelworker will one day spur further construction. If anything, my greatest hope is that this work serve as the edifice within which further study may be conducted – perhaps even by you, dear reader; again, nothing is ever really finished, and this building that has risen from soil to sky consists of dozens upon dozens of stories; feel free to furnish them lavishly.

Cory Vaillancourt,
August 2015

Few men are fortunate enough to be given the opportunity by their fellow citizens to preside over the rebuilding of the city they love. I've been given that opportunity – and I'll always be grateful to the voters of Erie.

Louis J. Tullio.

MAYOR

CONTENTS

ACKNOWLEDGMENTS

The author wishes to acknowledge the following individuals, all of whom made significant contributions to this work.

This book was edited by Ben Speggen of the Jefferson Educational Society, chapter by chapter, over half a year; analogous to a building inspector, Ben monitored progress, lent expertise, ensured integrity by asking the tough questions, and is perhaps the only reason this book is even readable.

Aside from the scholarship of the aforementioned Dr. William P. Garvey, Dr. Kyle Foust, and (soon-to-be Dr.) Ferki Ferati, important and invaluable insight was gained from the work of Mark Ostrowski and William C. Sennett, especially in regards to the Mike Cannavino era. Also due a hat-tip are the legions of newspaper reporters who, over the years, unwittingly created an enduring record of municipal government whilst performing their honorable trade with vigilance and respect.

Interviews conducted with Bob Brabender, Skip Cannavino, Pat Cappabianca, Richard Foht, John Horan, Pat Liebel, Edwin McKean, June Pintea, Fred Rush, Joyce Savocchio, John Tullio, Norma Tullio, and Ed Wellejus provided precious and irreplaceable testimony on Tullio's tenure by the very people who worked with, for, and against him.

Earleen Glaser – Reference Librarian and University Archivist at Mercyhurst University – saved untold hours of toil and trouble with her breadth of knowledge, and, interestingly, also monitored Ferati during his archival adventures, making her – like Garvey and Foust – one of the very few to have seen this work in progress over successive generations.

The production and creative teams that put this book in your hands were faced with the challenge of ensuring its integrity, as well as its aesthetic.

Alex Bieler did yeoman's work as the main proofreader and copy editor. Ian Willoughby's transcription and support as well as Mary Tredway's succinct-yet-elegant back cover copy both proved invaluable.

The book's look was masterminded by Higherglyphics CEO Todd Scalise; his art direction and general expertise coupled with Higherglyphics designer Kayla Nesselhauf's inspiring and dignified cover design as well as her heavily-researched font and style choices seamlessly compliment the subject matter in an engaging, visually pleasing way.

Even still, there are others who – possibly unbeknownst to them – advised, assisted, encouraged, inspired, supported, and/or sustained the author in some way during the fulfillment of this endeavor: Lisa Adams, Marcus Atkinson, Mallory Breon, Charles Brown, Betty Button, Caine Cortellino, Wendy Hall Elliott, John Elliott, Larry Franco, Captain Dan Geary, Howie Glover, Brian Graham, James "Gunner" Hall, David Hunter, Robert Jensen, Jeff Kazmer, Jason Lavery, Patrick Miller, Rob Oldham, Kate Philips, Mario Siano, Panhandle Slim, Jay Stevens, Rebecca Styn, Matt Texter, Steve Trohoske, Gerry Weiss, Adam Welsh, and Dr. Jim Wertz.

1

Tell Them I Want to Run

OCTOBER IN THE COMMONWEALTH OF PENNSYLVANIA IS ALWAYS A TIME of great change; it is a month of transition, during which the summery weather of months past continues to make occasional and welcomed appearances, but the wintry weather of months yet to come begins to dominate more and more, day by day.

Stretching more than 280 miles from east to west and 160 miles from north to south, Pennsylvania is a 46,055-square mile rectangular tabletop with one leg in the East, one in the Midwest, one in the frozen North, and one in Appalachia. This allows for great variation in climate amongst those who call themselves Pennsylvanians.

Erie, for example, lies tucked away in the northwestern part of Pennsylvania and is among the colder, snowier reaches of the commonwealth, often accumulating more than 100 inches of snow each year (owing mostly to its namesake Great Lake). Winter approaches early in Erie, and on Saturday, October 23, 1965, as most Erieites glanced forlornly at the coming week's forecast – which would bring temperatures in the 20s – Patricia Jane Liebel was frantically phoning Philadelphia.[1]

---

[1]Liebel, Patricia. Author interview with Patricia Liebel. 7 Jan. 2015.

Philadelphia, by contrast – situated in the southeastern part of Pennsylvania and more than 400 miles diagonally across the commonwealth from Erie – enjoys a slightly less arctic climate, owing to its more southerly location as well as the meteorologically moderating influences of the Atlantic Ocean. Winter comes later in Philadelphia, and on that mid-fall Saturday, the preceding days' highs in the low-70s had finally inched down to a pleasant 65 degrees.

Which made it, fortuitously, a perfect day for horseracing.

The Garden State Park Racetrack[2] (located just across the Delaware River from Philadelphia in nearby Cherry Hill, New Jersey) was built on the site of an old farm in 1942 and hosted some of the best thoroughbred racing on the Eastern Seaboard until decades of declining fortunes and the rise of Atlantic City as the "eastern Vegas" finally spelled its demise in 2001.

But in 1965 things were still in full gallop at the popular track, as several thousand patrons packed the noisy grandstand in anticipation of the afternoon's action – railbirds pawed racecards, broke-down bettors loudly weighed their odds, and conventioneers downed cheap beers while exuberantly fisting handfuls of cash through iron bars behind which bookies toiled and tabulated.

Then suddenly, in the middle of it all, above the din, a loudspeaker crackled to life with a most unusual announcement.

Some heads turned, and doubtless, some did not; but somewhere in that crowd, a man took notice of that announcement and began desperately searching for the track's house phone, where he'd worriedly answer the long-distance emergency call meant for him.[3]

Treading on discarded betting slips, snaking his way through the crowd of energetic revelers, and likely preparing himself for news of the worst sort, he finally found what he was looking for and picked up the receiver, whereupon he was promptly greeted by the anxious tones of Pat Liebel's voice.

"You've got to get home because Mike Cannavino's passed away," she said.

The voice on the other end responded in disbelief. "Oh my gosh,

[2]Strauss, Robert. "The Track Has Run Its Course". 29 Apr. 2001. New York Times. Accessed 27 Feb. 2015.
[3]Baker, Jeanne. Italian Politics. Mercyhurst University, 1970.

what happened?"

"I don't know the details of that," said Liebel of the heart attack that felled Erie Democratic Mayoral Candidate Cannavino just ten days before the November 2, 1965 Municipal General Election.

Liebel continued.

"The party wants to know if you want to run, because otherwise they've got to find somebody in a hurry."[4]

"I'll be home right away. Tell them," said Lou Tullio, "tell them I want to run."

---

[4] Liebel, Patricia. Author interview with Patricia Liebel. 7 Jan. 2015.

2

To Finish Out on Top

L ou Tullio must have jumped right into his car on that warm Saturday afternoon. Pointing it west and north, directly into the encroaching darkness and the steadily advancing cold front, he immediately began the long, drizzly journey back to Erie – a journey that would take him all night and give him ample time to ponder the practical implications of Mike Cannavino's untimely death.

Months earlier, after a bruising, hard-fought primary campaign, Erie voters had chosen the Democratic candidate they felt was best equipped to defeat vulnerable incumbent Republican Mayor Charles Williamson in the upcoming general election.

That candidate was a gregarious, well-known Italian-American Catholic, a prominent veteran of local Democratic politics who'd been a star football player in his youth and had then spent his life tirelessly building up political influence by glad-handing and back-slapping anyone within arm's reach at Erie's various festivals, firehouses, and funeral homes.

That candidate wasn't Tullio.

That candidate was Mike Cannavino – now the *late* Mike Cannavino – who in October 1965 was at the height of his political prowess and was all but certain to become Erie's next mayor.

Cannavino was born near Pittsburgh on November 15, 1907,[1] but moved with his family to Erie before 1915. By all accounts he was an intelligent, artistic, athletic young man, even having been offered a football scholarship to Yale University while attending Central High School.[2]

It is unknown why, but Cannavino never attended college, choosing instead to earn his degree from the school of hard knocks – the rough-and-tumble world of Erie Democratic ward politics in the first half of the 20th century.

Almost as soon as he began that endeavor, however, Cannavino suffered his first hard knock – at the age of 22, while travelling with friends to a football game in Pittsburgh, a car accident resulted in his leg being broken. It then became infected, and had to be amputated.[3]

Although Cannavino would go on to hobble around with a wooden leg for the rest of his life, it didn't appear to hold him back.

Indeed, at times Mike used his disability to his advantage as he circulated through Erie's diverse political scene, where he portrayed himself as an everyman-maverick who understood the suffering of "the little people," probably due to his own despair as a young man who had been visited by an unwanted and unwarranted calamity.

"We used to eat at the Hall's restaurant on the corner of Seventh and State," said Mike's nephew Carl "Skip" Cannavino. "He liked to go to the Maennerchor [Club], so he'd stop a car – just any car – and they would stop... he'd say 'My leg is killing me, can you drop me off at the Maennerchor?' [and] he would get a ride up, and a ride back... that was Mike."[4]

An underdog who never married but instead was wedded to politics, Cannavino's fledgling political career began at the tender age of 24 in 1931 when he was elected Third Ward Assessor – a position now known as District Judge that Cannavino would go on to hold for six

---

[1] "Mike A. Cannavino obituary." Erie Morning News 25 Oct. 1965: sec. B p. 2.
[2] Foust, Kyle. "Why Lou Tullio: How Erie's Most Powerful Mayor Came to Power." Journal of Erie Studies (2003): 57-75.
[3] Ibid.
[4] Cannavino, Skip. Author Interview with Skip Cannavino. 8 Jan. 2015.

years.[5] After failed attempts at winning a city council seat in 1937 and 1939, he became the lone Democrat and lone Italian-American on the Erie School Board in 1944. From there, Cannavino continued in his relentless and exuberant acquisition of political capital.

Uncle Mike, Skip said, also visited wakes and funerals whether he knew the deceased or not[6] – an acceptable political practice at the time that is rather questionable today. So determined to make an impression was Cannavino that if parking wasn't readily available he would park his car in the middle of the street,[7] rush in, pay his respects, and – in what was also an acceptable political practice at the time that is rather questionable today – leave a small sum of cash with the family before rushing back out to his illegally-parked car.[8]

Skip also recalled a particularly poor family that Mike, who owned a tavern, would often assist. "They had like 13 kids, and every Christmas, he was there to give them a basket of food or money or whatever."[9]

Generous to a fault, Mike did that type of thing "quite often," Skip said.[10]

Outgoing and jovial, Mike was also an amateur magician who performed for children in area schools, and was involved in local youth baseball organizations as well. There seemed to be no segment of Erie with which "Magic Mike" could not ingratiate himself – he knew exactly how best to appeal to whatever crowd happened to be assembled, regardless of age, sex, or race; Skip recounted a particular speech Mike delivered on the Lower East Side sometime in the early 1960s.

"They treat me pretty bad at City Hall," said Mike to the overwhelmingly African-American crowd. "They call me a cripple. [But] do you know what they call you? 'Niggers!'" [11]

"They all clapped," despite the inflammatory nature of the slur, Skip said, "because they knew – they knew he was sincere."

Mike's sincerity aside, he was also possessed of a seemingly unquenchable lust for authority and power. He ran for mayor in the Sep-

---

[5] Erie Hall of Fame. "Mike Cannavino." Accessed 27 Feb. 2015.
[6] Cannavino, Skip. Author Interview with Skip Cannavino. 8 Jan. 2015.
[7] Liebel, Patricia. Author interview with Patricia Liebel. 7 Jan. 2015.
[8] Cannavino, Skip. Author Interview with Skip Cannavino. 8 Jan. 2015.
[9] Ibid.
[10] Ibid.
[11] Ibid.

tember 1947 Democratic Municipal Primary and put on a respectable showing, but City Councilman Sherman Hickey, Jr. bested him by a slim margin. Hickey would go on to defeat Republican candidate Gail Ross in November of that year, but died in office not long after assuming control.[12]

The Erie County Democratic Party, Cannavino alleged, wasn't quite as neutral as it should have been during his primary with Hickey, so when Councilman Joseph Martin won the special election held to fill the remainder of the late Mayor Hickey's term in 1948, Cannavino was chosen to replace Martin on council as a fence-mending measure.[13]

Although Cannavino was unable to retain the appointed seat in that year's regular election, he set his sights on recapturing it, which he did in 1949. And while higher office was certainly still his goal, Cannavino now had a more effective and enduring means by which he could build his political network.

♦ ♦ ♦

Cannavino would end up serving three terms on council, earning himself wide-ranging local clout and the confidence to run for Pennsylvania Secretary of Internal Affairs – a statewide office – in 1959.[14] He was defeated but not discouraged, and again set his sights on becoming mayor of Erie.

The Erie Municipal Election of 1961 would become the most pivotal in Erie's history. Prior to 1961, the city of Erie had what is known as the "councilmatic" form of government, so named because of the powerful role of the city council. The mayor was but one of five city councilmen, each with one vote, and all with responsibility to lead one of five city departments.[15]

Those departments – Finance, Parks, Public Affairs, Streets, and Safety – operated as virtual fiefdoms, ruled by modern-day lords who regularly competed against each other for precious and scarce resources

---

[12] Foust, Kyle. "Why Lou Tullio: How Erie's Most Powerful Mayor Came to Power." *Journal of Erie Studies* 32 no. 2, 2003: 57-75.
[13] Ibid.
[14] Ibid.
[15] Ibid.

from the city budget. Employees of the various departments were hired, fired, promoted, and demoted nearly at will by councilmen in a well-oiled machine whose gears were greased by political patronage.

"Patronage" was and is a means of acquiring or maintaining political power by steering government jobs and contracts to friends or supporters. It's a powerful tool that entrenches incumbents and enriches a select few, and it's been practiced in the United States from the very beginning.

As colonial Americans ventured west and established settlements on the periphery of their infant nation (which was, in reality, just a thin strip of land directly adjacent to the Atlantic Ocean) throughout the late 1700s, those settlers brought with them more than just their worldly possessions – they also brought with them their ethnic and religious identities. And Americans of that time – or, at least, Americans of the time with the means and the ability to seek their fortunes in distant, unforgiving lands – were overwhelmingly Protestant, and of Canadian, English, Irish, or Scottish descent.

Consequently, in many towns outside of the original 13 Colonies (like Erie) the "old order" – those first settlers who stepped into an economic and political power vacuum and became, by necessity, moguls and mayors – consisted of what are popularly known today as "Yankees."

By contrast, as the tired, poor, huddled masses of Europe yearning to breathe free arrived in successive waves to look upon the lamp beside the golden door during the 1800s, they were overwhelmingly Catholic, and of Italian, Irish, German, or Polish descent.

Thusly was the stage set; very generally, the history of political conflict in the Eastern United States through the 1970s can be fairly characterized as the struggle for influence between established Anglo-Protestants and newly-arrived European Catholics.

As these immigrants disbursed throughout what would become the American Midwest, they sought economic opportunity and political influence, much like those who had originally established the towns in which these new Americans would settle.

Finding those seats of power occupied by families who had a decades-long head start on them, these uneducated Italian, Irish, and Polish Catholics began in the more humble rungs of blue-collar society. They became cooks and clerks and cops and bakers; their focus, as newcomers, was first on survival and second on ensuring for their descendants access to the full advantages of the American educational and economic system that they themselves didn't have as children growing up in a fragmented, famine-blighted, war-torn Europe.

Over successive generations, as the sons and daughters of cooks and clerks and cops and bakers became restauranteurs and retailers and politicians and bankers, their populations grew in both number and wealth. Meanwhile, the Yankee population remained flat, and by the 1900s, began to dwindle.[16] And then all at once, the immense momentum of history was upon them.

Faced with an eroding electoral base due to a demographic shift of colossal proportions, the Yankees' only solution was to court the support of – and cede some small slice of power to – these rising ethnic minorities. That power was disbursed through patronage jobs.

A skilled political operator, Cannavino clearly recognized and exploited his power to disburse patronage, as did others on council.

Under the councilmatic system, councilmen decided who got what. Friends got jobs and promotions – jobs and promotions that paid for a tiny piece of the American dream that transformed yesterday's impoverished immigrants into tomorrow's local leaders.

Those grateful friends reciprocated by supporting their patrons politically – by voting, by encouraging their family, friends, and acquaintances to vote, or by making campaign contributions.

The ungrateful or downright oppositional got passed over for promotion, demoted, fired, or were never hired in the first place.

However, in 1959 Erie voters had approved a change from the councilmatic system to what was called the "strong mayor" form of government,[17] wherein mayors taking office after 1961 would *appoint* the directors of those city departments, ultimately assuming all that clout for themselves in the name of "efficiency," and leaving council to concentrate solely on legislation rather than administration.

The demise of the councilmatic system would not eliminate patronage, but instead concentrate it in the mayor, cutting council out of the deal. Of course, council members would retain some influence, but after 1961, they'd have to ask the mayor for it.

---

[16] Garvey, William P. PhD. The Ethnic Factor in Erie Politics. PhD. diss., University of Pittsburgh, 1973.

[17] Sennett, William C. "The 1961 Erie Mayoral Election." Journal of Erie Studies 32 no. 2, 2003: 29-46.

With the wide-open days of patronage coming to a close for Councilman Cannavino – who had served as director of finance, director of streets, and director of safety over his three terms from 1952 to 1965 – he had seemingly assembled everything he needed to become Erie's first strong mayor, and just in time.

▰ ▰ ▰

There was one significant obstacle, however – incumbent Democratic Mayor Art Gardner.

Gardner, 47, was a Gannon College graduate, former city assessor, and wealthy businessman dealing in real estate and was appointed mayor in 1955 in the wake of the bribery scandal that resulted in the conviction of Mayor Thomas Flatley.[18] Gardner was then elected to full terms in 1955 and 1959, and sought reelection in 1961.

Mayor Gardner and Councilman Cannavino were joined in the Democratic Municipal Primary by Julian Polaski, a veteran state legislator and de-facto political leader of Erie's East-side Polish community.[19]

Polaski's entry into the race remains somewhat mystifying; he was closely associated with Cannavino, so much so that his sister served as Cannavino's secretary.[20]

To Polaski's credit, he had been a viciously vocal opponent of Mayor Gardner, however, the failure of Cannavino and Polaski to work together against their mutual foe would come back to haunt both of them.[21]

After an ugly campaign full of smears and jeers, Mayor Gardner emerged as the victor of the 1961 Democratic Primary with 10,915 votes to Cannavino's 10,775. Polaski had stolen 3,926 votes – the overwhelming majority of which would have gone to Cannavino, as few who had endorsed Polaski's anti-Gardner rhetoric would have, in his absence, voted for Gardner.[22]

City Republicans, on the other hand, were just as much in disarray as their Democratic counterparts.

---

[18] Ibid.
[19] Ibid.
[20] Ibid.
[21] Ibid.
[22] Ibid.

Erie County Republican Party Chairman John English – who had lost to Mayor Gardner in the 1959 Municipal Election – again threw his hat into the ring. Intrigues, however, abounded; a youthful dissident faction of the local Republican Party splintered from the organization and pushed longtime educator Charles Williamson, who was an assistant principal at East High School, to oppose English.[23]

On Municipal Primary Election Day, May 16, 1961, Williamson – who'd lost to English in the 1959 Republican Mayoral Primary – thrashed English by a nearly 3-to-1 margin,[24] and the general election field was confirmed – Gardner versus Williamson.

◢ ◢ ◢

But Mike Cannavino wasn't out of the picture just yet.

Despite Cannavino's reputation as a jovial, endearing gentleman, he also had a dark side that he kept well-hidden from his adoring public.

Cannavino always saw himself as a man made in the mold of legendary New York City Mayor Fiorello LaGuardia – that is, as an "incurable insurgent,"[25] a fighter against the forces of perceived evil who was more than happy to break some eggs in the making of his perfect omelet. Cannavino even portrayed LaGuardia in a stage production of *Fiorello* at the Erie Playhouse, and was so popular that the production's run had to be extended.[26] He relished his identity as a political rebel who could be crude and unpolished at times, but that identity – coupled with his narrow defeat in what was probably the aging rogue's last, best chance at becoming Erie's mayor – revealed aspects of Cannavino's personality that painted a stark contrast to his carefully groomed public image.

After his devastating primary loss to Gardner, Cannavino refused to concede the election.[27] A few weeks later, in early June, Cannavino initiated a formal recount against his fellow Democrat, alleging misdeeds and miscounts; unfortunately for Cannavino, this recount not only failed to uncover any misdeeds on the part of Gardner or election officials, it uncovered only minor miscounts that actually *increased*

---

[23] Ibid.
[24] Ibid.
[25] Brodsky, Alyn. The Great Mayor. New York: St. Martin's Press, 2003 (75).
[26] Foust, Kyle. "Why Lou Tullio: How Erie's Most Powerful Mayor Came to Power."
   Journal of Erie Studies 32 no. 2, 2003: 57-75.
[27] Ibid.

Gardner's margin of victory from 140 to 147 votes.[28]

Not yet content to let the matter drop and rejoin the party faithful in their greater goal of returning Gardner to office, Cannavino's machinations escalated one week after the failed recount. Cannavino refused to support his fellow Democrat Gardner and began actively campaigning against him by mutating his own campaign apparatus, "Committee for Cannavino," into a much different entity, called "Democratic Boosters for Williamson."[29]

Cannavino's conniving worked; Williamson, a Republican, pulled off a shocking upset victory against a two-term incumbent Democratic mayor, despite the fact that the city's 40,000 registered Democrats outnumbered Republicans by 15,000.[30]

Williamson's margin of 2,569 votes – 26,583 to 24,014 for Gardner[31] – was *just* slim enough to validate the theory that the Democratic Boosters for Williamson made an impact that would deny Gardner his chance to become Erie's first strong mayor.

But Cannavino's disloyalty to his own party might not have just been sour grapes from a desperate, defeated man – a larger strategy may have been at work.

Speculation[32] quickly emerged that Cannavino was already lining himself up to run for mayor again in 1965 and Williamson – the first elected Republican mayor in almost 20 years – would certainly be an easier target than Gardner, whose masterful manipulation of Erie's media and mostly-cooperative city council would have made him, after four years of strong rule, nearly undefeatable.

Whatever the reason, only time would tell if the road Cannavino had chosen would deliver him to his now far-off destination.

Tullio's destination was, however, drawing ever closer.

---

[28] Ibid.
[29] Garvey, William P. PhD. The Ethnic Factor in Erie Politics. PhD. diss., University of Pittsburgh, 1973.
[30] Foust, Kyle. "Why Lou Tullio: How Erie's Most Powerful Mayor Came to Power." Journal of Erie Studies 32 no. 2, 2003: 57-75.
[31] Garvey, William P. PhD. The Ethnic Factor in Erie Politics. PhD. diss., University of Pittsburgh, 1973.
[32] Sennett, William C. "The 1961 Erie Mayoral Election." Journal of Erie Studies 32 no. 2, 2003 29-46.

▟ ▟ ▟

That warm Saturday afternoon in the fall of 1965 had become a damp chilly midnight somewhere in the wilds of Central Pennsylvania; with Philadelphia several hundred miles behind him, Tullio probably couldn't help but reflect on the similarities between himself and Mike Cannavino as he stared out the rain-spotted car windows at the streetlamps shining their odd orange glow on the rain-slicked pavement of the now mostly-complete Interstate 80.

Tullio and Cannavino were both gregarious, well-known Italian-American Catholics. They were both prominent veterans of local Democratic politics. They'd both been a star football players in high school. They'd both spent their lives building up political influence.

And they both thought they were ready to be Erie's next mayor.

They were probably both right, but for reasons they weren't consciously considering.

In 1951, Sociologist and Yale Professor Jerome K. Myers authored a pioneering and now widely-cited study that suggested that ethnic minorities entered into and advanced through the ranks of patronage jobs in direct proportion to their importance to the old order's hold on power.[33]

Myers also theorized that eventually a time would come when those minorities favored by the old order in such a manner would become powerful enough to overtake the ruling coalition, and that the timing of these ethnic power shifts correlated well with the amount of these ethnic minorities holding non-elected patronage positions.

His model holds up well in many cities across the nation, including Erie.

The Germans were the first ethnic minority to overtake the old order; from 1899 to 1924, both Protestant and Catholic Germans exclusively occupied the mayoralty.[34]

Irish immigration to the United States peaked in 1851,[35] and by

[33] Garvey, William P. PhD. The Ethnic Factor in Erie Politics. PhD. diss., University of Pittsburgh, 1973.
[34] Ibid.
[35] Spartacus Educational. Immigration Peak Years. n.d. 31 Jan. 2015.

1920, they held 20 percent of patronage positions in Erie despite being just 8 percent of the population; they were at the height of their power just as they were electing their first mayor in 1931, and wielded this power until the Flatley scandal in 1954.[36]

After a brief interregnum brought on by the chaotic state of city government after Flatley's removal, Gardner's appointment, and Williamson's aberration, the Italians were finally ready for their turn.

Their emigration to the United States had peaked in 1907,[37] and although they comprised only 11 percent of the population of Erie in 1960, they held 18 percent of patronage positions – a strong sign of socioeconomic maturation in this late-arriving ethnic group. Also by 1960, Catholics made up approximately 48 percent of Erie's population, up from just 29 percent in 1910.[38]

A hard-working immigrant named Anthony[39] was among this new wave of Italian Catholics, but the surname he brought with him – Tullio – was an ancient one, derived from "Tullius," and translating roughly to "one who leads."[40] Arriving in the United States in the early 1900s, he settled on the east side of Erie, working as a cement contractor.

Once suitably established, he sent for his wife, Ersilia Nardoni, who he'd married after growing up next to her family in a former convent-turned-apartment building 60 miles southeast of Rome in Vallecorsa, Italy.[41]

Anthony learned to speak English out of necessity – unlike his wife – and became a successful contractor and businessman until he went bankrupt during the Great Depression. He then labored for the Works Progress Administration, an expansive New Deal program that employed almost 4 million men and women in the construction of public

---

[36] Garvey, William P. PhD. The Ethnic Factor in Erie Politics. PhD. diss., University of Pittsburgh, 1973.

[37] Spartacus Educational. Immigration Peak Years. n.d. 31 Jan. 2015.

[38] Garvey, William P. PhD. The Ethnic Factor in Erie Politics. PhD. diss., University of Pittsburgh, 1973.

[39] Tullio, John and Norma. Author interview with John and Norma Tullio. 15 Jan. 2015.

[40] Tullio. Accessed 9 Nov. 2014. <http://www.spokenhere.com/tag/tullio>.

[41] Tullio, John and Norma. Author interview with John and Norma Tullio. 15 Jan. 2015.

works by 1936.[42]

Money was tight, and Anthony and Ersilia soon found themselves with many hungry mouths to feed; among them, six girls – Elizabeth, Amelia, Rose, Marie, Lee, and Jean – and two boys, John and Louis.

Louis Joseph Tullio entered this world on May 17, 1916.[43] He was born in Erie, as were all of his siblings.[44]

"What I remember most about him of course was that he went to Cathedral Prep [high school]," said John Tullio, Lou's younger (by 9 years) brother. "He was a football player."[45]

A decent student, Lou was captain of the Prep football team in 1934.[46] He played fullback and linebacker, and led the team to a 6-3 record while earning All-Scholastic team honors after the season.[47]

Although being a football player was central to his identity as a young man, he was also a bit of a prankster.

"He was going to Prep, and someone had given him a big pair of false shoes that fit over his feet," John said. "So he came in the house, and he looked really tired, and my mother – who was a rather stern woman, in fact she ran the family – came in and he was walking real slow, you know, with those false shoes on, and my mother says 'What's wrong?'"

Spying Lou's comically oversized shoes, Ersilia erupted. "She looked at him, and oh my God, she practically clubbed him," said John.[48]

Lou survived his mother's wrath in decent enough shape to earn a football scholarship to College of the Holy Cross in Worcester, Massachusetts.[49] He played fullback and guard, and graduated in 1939 with a Bachelor's Degree in Business Administration.[50]

---

[42] Works Progress Administration. WPA Workers Handbook. 1936. Accessed 30 Mar. 2015.

[43] Howard, Pat. "Erieites express their views of Lou Tullio as man, mayor." Erie Daily Times. 17 April 1990: sec. B, p. 1.

[44] Tullio, John and Norma. Author interview with John and Norma Tullio. 15 Jan. 2015.

[45] Ibid.

[46] Cuneo, Pat. "The Sportsman: A look at how athletic coaching, competition forged the legend." Erie Morning News. 18 Apr. 1990: [special section] p. 11.

[47] Ibid.

[48] Tullio, John and Norma. Author interview with John and Norma Tullio. 15 Jan. 2015.

[49] Cuneo, Pat. "The Sportsman: A look at how athletic coaching, competition forged the legend." Erie Morning News. 18 Apr. 1990: [special section] p. 11.

[50] Pinksy, Jeff. "Area mourns loss of Lou Tullio." Erie Morning News 18 Apr. 1990: sec. 1 p. 1.

During his stint at Holy Cross, Lou – a strapping,[51] light-haired,[52] well-dressed[53] young bachelor – met Mary Cecelia McHale.

Mary Cecelia – known as Ceil – was the only child of John Patrick and Mary Cecilia McHale, an Irish Catholic couple who owned and operated a large dairy farm built in 1792 about seven miles northwest of Worcester, in Paxton, Massachusetts.[54]

"She was a typically bred New England woman, my mother was," said June Pintea, Lou's daughter. "Never heard her swear. Now she might have, but to the best of my knowledge as a young person, and even as an adult, she never raised her voice."

An only child, Ceil was well-doted on by her father. "He went into Worcester one Christmas and he bought her this absolutely beautiful doll," June said. "She was a window display. And he said, 'Would you sell that doll?' because my mother was just fascinated with it. 'No,' [the store owner said]. 'It's part of the props, part of the display.' But he went back after Christmas, and he bought that doll for her."[55]

Travelling miles into the city during working hours was a special and difficult trip for a busy farmer of the time, but John McHale "showered love" on Ceil, and when she wanted something that he agreed with, he'd make sure she got it.[56]

"He was a pretty tough guy, too, but also very gentle," said June of her father. "So there were a lot of similarities between Grandpa McHale and my father. You had to be tough in those days to run a farm, and my father was tough in another way, but they were both gentle men. And I think that's probably what attracted my mother to my father."[57]

Ceil was a unique woman for her time. She was somewhat sheltered, but was also a college graduate. She was an avid horseback rider, but had never stepped foot into the cow barn.[58] She was a studious, shy, and retiring country girl with model-quality looks and a thick Irish brogue[59]

[51] Tullio, John and Norma. Author interview with John and Norma Tullio. 15 Jan. 2015.
[52] Cappabianca, Pat. Author interview with Pat Cappabianca. 5 Jan. 2015.
[53] Pintea, June. Author interview with June Pintea. 22 Jan. 2015.
[54] Ibid.
[55] Ibid.
[56] Ibid.
[57] Ibid.
[58] Ibid.
[59] Tullio, John and Norma. Author interview with John and Norma Tullio. 15 Jan. 2015.

who fell in love with and married a real Erie guy – a rough-around-the-edges Italian city slicker and college business student who also happened to play semi-pro football for the Providence Steamrollers.[60]

After marrying, Lou and Ceil lived with her parents in Paxton; far from being a fish out of water, he put his business degree right to work, and convinced the McHales to let him open up a milk vending operation based on their farm.[61]

Thus, this American Tullius – who would eventually lead a small Midwestern city for nearly a quarter of a century – began his professional career inauspiciously, as a humble milkman.

"I think he liked the fact that he started off as a milkman," June said. "Here's a guy who got a scholarship to The College of the Holy Cross, and was the son of immigrant parents, and here he was working on a farm. I think he liked being called a milkman during that period of time, and later in life he would often joke and tell stories about how he started off as the milkman."[62]

▪ ▪ ▪

The economic recovery Anthony Tullio had awaited finally emerged, but brought with it worldwide warfare; as his business picked up again in Erie, Anthony's oldest son – a married, college-educated, successful entrepreneur and father now living in Massachusetts – was called away to fight in 1942.

Lou served in the United States Navy in the pacific theater – eventually attaining the rank of Lieutenant – and didn't permanently return home to Paxton until 1946.[63]

"I didn't see him until I was three years old," said June, who was conceived while her father was home on leave and born while her father was half a world away. "Of course, I thought he was a stranger... I kept

[60] Cuneo, Pat. "The Sportsman: A look at how athletic coaching, competition forged the legend." Erie Morning News. 18 Apr. 1990: [special section] p. 11.
[61] Pintea, June. Author interview with June Pintea. 22 Jan. 2015.
[62] Ibid.
[63] Ibid.

saying 'Who is this strange man in the farmhouse?' And my grandpa would say, 'That's your daddy,' and I'd say, 'Ohhh!' I thought grandpa was my daddy."[64]

Delivering milk and farming with his young family may have been just fine for Tullio, but it wouldn't be long before he again focused on football.

He began teaching and coaching 60 miles away at Saint Anselm College in Manchester, New Hampshire, as well as at St. Peter High School in Worcester.[65] But when the opportunity arose for Lou to bring his wife and three daughters back to Erie in 1947, he sold the Springdale Dairy – begun with $500 of borrowed money – for $10,000[66] and moved to what June called the Tullio clan's "compound," a collection of several houses all owned by family members near 25th and Brandes streets on Erie's east side.

His first jobs after he returned to Erie were all football-related; he served as the Cathedral Prep junior varsity football coach and assistant coach at East High School. After that, he became the athletic director and head football Coach at Gannon College (now University) in 1949, where he guided the Knights to a 16-2 record over two seasons – during one of which their opponents couldn't even muster a single point. He was also head coach of the Erie Vets, a semi-pro football team that played their home games at Erie's Veterans Memorial Stadium, in 1950.[67]

Gannon eliminated its football program in 1951 due to budgetary constraints, and the versatile Tullio stayed on as the college's basketball coach until 1956, when football again drew his attention. He left Gannon to become the head coach at Academy High School. Also in 1956, Tullio was promoted to assistant director of health and physical education for the Erie School District, a position he would hold for four years, during which time he earned his Master's Degree in Physical Education from Boston University in 1958.[68]

---

[64] Ibid.

[65] Cuneo, Pat. "The Sportsman: A look at how athletic coaching, competition forged the legend." Erie Morning News. 18 Apr. 1990: [special section] p. 11.

[66] Garvey, William P. PhD. The Ethnic Factor in Erie Politics. PhD. diss., University of Pittsburgh, 1973.

[67] Cuneo, Pat. "The Sportsman: A look at how athletic coaching, competition forged the legend." Erie Morning News. 18 Apr. 1990: [special section] p. 11.

[68] Ibid.

This job with the school district would put Tullio in position to capitalize on the unexpected 1960 departure of Art Logan – the powerful Secretary-Business Manager of the Erie School District who'd been given a position of Pennsylvania deputy secretary of streets and highways by newly-minted Governor David L. Lawrence.[69]

Counterintuitively, the most powerful, patronage-rich position in all of Erie was not a city councilman or "strong" mayor – it was the Secretary-Business Manager of the Erie School Board, which oversaw nearly 1,000 jobs and a $12 million annual budget that was larger than *the entire City of Erie's.*

If anything, Tullio's service as the secretary-business manager of the Erie School District in this position left him just as powerful as Cannavino, if not more so.

◢ ◢ ◢

Politically, their roads intersected in 1965, Cannavino's and Tullio's; as long and as winding and as overlapping and as rainy and as sunny as they sometimes were, both men's journeys had led them to a junction. They were at the height of their power within their ethnic minorities at the same time as their ethnic minority – the Italians – were at the height of *their* power.

The crafty Cannavino – alluding to his long career in politics and, at the age of 57, his impending mortality – had implored primary voters to choose him over Tullio so he could "finish out on top."[70]

They did.

Cannavino, however – the outgoing, generous man who spent his life fighting for the "little people" and trying to help everyone and anyone he could (including himself) – died broke and alone just ten days before the election.

Such was the reason for Pat Liebel's frantic phone call of Saturday, October 23 to Philly and also the reason for Tullio's sudden departure

[69] Foust, Kyle. "Why Lou Tullio: How Erie's Most Powerful Mayor Came to Power." Journal of Erie Studies 32 no. 2, 2003: 57-75

[70] Ibid.

from the school district business he'd been attending there – if the Erie County Democratic Party didn't decide on a replacement candidate in short order, they'd have no one to blame for four more years of Mayor Williamson, the Republican aberration.

Now, on Sunday, October 24, 1965, after a long night of travel from warm, sunny Philadelphia to damp, chilly Erie, Tullio had finally made it home. It was 4:30 in the morning, and a man named Robert Horn was standing in his driveway.[71]

Incidentally, Cannavino's death didn't prevent his long-held dream from coming true; in a cruel twist of fate, Mike Cannavino did indeed finish out on top.

Just days after his death, in an unprecedented act brought about at the behest of Tullio, Mayor Williamson declared Cannavino honorary mayor of Erie.[72]

---

[71] Ibid.
[72] Rogowski, Bill. "Party Committeeman Make Vote Unanimous." Erie Morning News. 25 Oct. 1965: sec. 1 p. 1.

3

Lucky Lou

S UNDAY, OCTOBER 24, 1965 WOULD BE A DAY FULL OF BLUSTER IN ERIE; rainy and windy with a high in the mid-40s, the weather was not atypical for the season, but was perhaps appropriate for the decidedly atypical meeting about to take place.

The temperature had dropped into the mid-30s as 144 members of the Erie County Democratic Committee descended on the county courthouse; although the headline on the front page of the *Erie Times-News*, in large type, said "CITY MOURNS MIKE,"[1] the subhead was perhaps a better barometer of the political climate.

In smaller type, it read "Committee to Fill Vacancy."[2]

They didn't have to; they could have taken their chances and left Mike Cannavino on the ballot, beseeching voters with an emotional appeal to let Cannavino "finish out on top," and then appointing a mayor later, if he posthumously defeated Mayor Williamson.

[1] Minegar, Garth. "City Mourns Mike." Erie Times News. Oct. 24, 1965, sec. 1, p. 1.
[2] Ibid.

Lou Tullio's supporters, however, had been pressing the Democratic Party[3] for Tullio to take Cannavino's place since learning of his death the day before.

Among those supporters was Pat Liebel. After graduating from Mercyhurst College (now University), Liebel got a job with the Erie School District as the influential Art Logan's secretary. She worked for Erie School District Secretary-Business Manager Logan for 12 years, during which time she first met Tullio when he became the assistant director of health and physical education in 1956. When Logan left to take an appointed position in the Lawrence administration in 1960, Tullio took his place, and Liebel continued in her old job with her new boss.[4]

"I was already in the chair, so he kept me," Liebel said.

It was the beginning of a close personal and professional relationship between the two that would go on to last 30 years.

Appropriately, it was Liebel who first notified Tullio of Cannavino's death, and as Lou motored home through the night, Liebel was already rallying the remnants of the previously-defeated Tullio's army of supporters. It had only been five months since Tullio's loss to Cannavino; consequently, Liebel found "pretty much everything in order" to begin advancing again.[5]

After all, Tullio *was* the logical choice to replace Cannavino, and not just because of the recent rise of the Italian Catholics in Erie; Tullio had been the only candidate to oppose Cannavino in the primary, and had only lost to him by a slim margin.

But there was bitter opposition from some of Cannavino's supporters, who felt cheated by his death; they, too, expected to benefit from the ascension of their patron to the mayoralty, and when he died, those expectations died along with him.

However, much of the opposition to Tullio from Cannavino supporters was because they just plain didn't like him. From their perspective, there was much to dislike.

The hierarchical nature of patronage politics was a slave to rank and custom akin to a Ponzi scheme; party members were encouraged to pay

---

[3] Ibid.
[4] Liebel, Patricia. Author interview with Patricia Liebel. 7 Jan. 2015.
[5] Ibid.

their dues patiently by working for and contributing to candidates until, one day, if they labored diligently enough and played their cards right, it would be their turn to ask for favors or to run for office. Interlopers were generally scorned, and Tullio – having spent years away from the Erie political scene in Massachusetts – was perceived as one of them.[6] Cannavino had paid his dues; Tullio, despite his rapid, meteoric rise, had not.

"The Italians were very upset with him," Liebel said, referring to the man who dared oppose the anointed Cannavino.[7]

Tullio's rift with the West Side Italians was deepened further by his residency on Erie's East Side; the ethnic conflicts in Erie politics have never existed solely as some abstract, scholarly notion far removed from the grimy barrooms and glitzy ballrooms of the city – these conflicts have always overlaid the city's grid-like system of political wards, imbuing all six of them with distinctly different ethnic character and political dispositions.

In June 1795, the city of Erie was surveyed by Andrew Ellicott at the behest of the Pennsylvania General Assembly.[8] Ellicott – who was called upon in 1792 to complete Washington, D.C.'s master plan after Pierre Charles L'Enfant's dismissal by President George Washington – laid out streets running east and west, which were aligned parallel to the shore of Presque Isle Bay and were numbered low to high as they progressed south, away from the shore. Streets running north and south were aligned perpendicular to the shore and were named after trees, plants, and ethnicities.

State Street is where east and west come together.

On the east side of State Street (see fig. 1), the First Ward runs from the water south to Eighth Street. From Eighth Street south to 18th Street lies the Second Ward, and from 18th Street south to Grandview Boulevard sits the Fifth Ward.

On the west side of State Street, the Fourth Ward runs from the water south to Eighth Street. From Eighth Street south to 18th Street lies the Third Ward, and from 18th Street south to Grandview Boulevard sits the Sixth Ward.

---

[6] Rush, Fred. Author interview with Fred Rush. 14 Jan. 2015.
[7] Liebel, Patricia. Author interview with Patricia Liebel. 7 Jan. 2015.
[8] Wellejus, Ed. *Erie: Chronicle of a Great Lakes City.* Woodland Hills, CA: Windsor Publications, 1980.

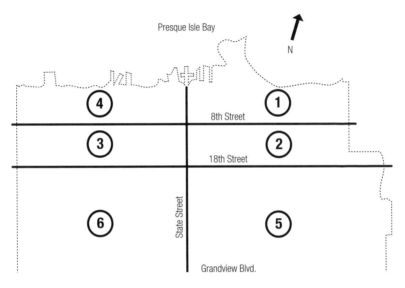

(*fig. 1*) The City of Erie's Electoral Wards.

All six of these wards were dominated by Yankees and Germans in 1900,[9] but by 1960, the Italians, Irish, and Polish challenged that dominance in all wards but one – the wealthy west side lakefront Fourth Ward, where Yankees and Germans made up 75 percent of the population. Party-wise, the Fourth Ward was the last bastion of Republican strength left in Erie, and voted for Republican mayors in each election since 1920. The rest of the city regularly voted Democrat.

The First, Second, and Fifth Wards – all east of State Street – were heavily Polish. In the Second Ward, the Poles were 49 percent of the population; their power extended to the north in the First Ward, where they made up 28 percent, and also to the south in the Fifth Ward, where they still represented 20 percent of the population.[10]

West of State Street, 18th Street cuts right through the heart of Little Italy. North of 18th Street in the Third Ward, Italians made up 19 percent of the population; south of it, in the Sixth Ward, they made up 20 percent.[11]

Cannavino resided on West 21st Street,[12] in the Sixth Ward, and demonstrated his power over the West Side Italians in 1961; his "Democratic Boosters for Williamson" organization deftly persuaded the Third and Sixth Wards to vote Republican, something they'd done just three times since 1920.

Tullio, on the other hand, resided outside the Italian seat of power, in the Polish-dominated Fifth Ward – which, to Cannavino supporters, made Tullio not only a line-jumper, but also an outsider.

It would also one day make and keep him mayor.

◢ ◢ ◢

In mid-November 1964, Democrat Lyndon Johnson had just defeated Republican Barry Goldwater in the U.S. Presidential Election; "Baby Love" by the Supremes was atop the pop music charts, Elvis Presley's *Roustabout* was the box office number-one movie, Sammy Davis, Jr. was on TV's *The Ed Sullivan Show*, and Lou Tullio – having neither held nor sought elective office before – was about to launch his

---

[9] Garvey, William P. PhD. The Ethnic Factor in Erie Politics. PhD. diss, University of Pittsburgh, 1973.

[10] Ibid.

[11] Ibid.

[12] Cannavino, Skip. Author interview with Skip Cannavino. 8 Jan 2015.

primary campaign for mayor of the City of Erie.

Mike Cannavino would wait until February 1965 to make his announcement. Within a day he suffered a substantial heart attack that would sideline him for almost a month,[13] all of which gave the underdog Tullio nearly four months to secure endorsements, hold rallies, and compete for campaign contributions practically uncontested.

Despite Cannavino's convalescence, his organization continued to work on his behalf, albeit with slightly diminished effectiveness due to Cannavino's unavailability. To remedy this, Cannavino resumed campaigning – against the advice of his physicians[14] – in mid-March, just two months before the May 18 Municipal Primary Election. His campaign slogan was, "I like Mike."

As the campaign began in earnest, real differences in these very similar men started to emerge above and beyond the geographical peculiarities of their supporters.

Tullio had a Master's Degree; Cannavino did not. Tullio had been a successful small-business owner; for the most part, Cannavino had not. Tullio was in decent health and enjoyed golf, swimming, and handball; Cannavino was enfeebled. Tullio favored a grand and aspirational view of Erie's role in the larger world,[15] but Cannavino rested on his "big small town" philosophy of neighborly cooperation.

Consequently, Tullio enjoyed better relations with Erie's intellectuals and business community than Cannavino did. Tullio also had the confidence of voters that he was in good enough shape to serve out his term as mayor.

Conversely, Cannavino's relative lack of education and sophistication continued to endear him to the "little people" he so often spoke of and fought for, and his recent health-related woes were merely another challenge he would eventually overcome, just as he had done with the car accident that resulted in his leg's amputation more than 35 years prior.

These important differences were voiced not by the candidates themselves, however; they were whispered in hushed tones throughout the city. Privately, Tullio was portrayed by detractors as opportunistic,

---

[13] Foust, Kyle. "Why Lou Tullio: How Erie's Most Powerful Mayor Came to Power." Journal of Erie Studies, vol. 32, no. 2 (2003): 57-75.
[14] Ibid.
[15] Ibid.

snobby, wealthy, and over-educated. Cannavino was portrayed as a poor simpleton on death's door. None of it was completely accurate, but all of it held a kernel of truth.

Publicly, both men distanced themselves from the mudslinging, which began to intensify along with the campaign in early May.

With Election Day drawing closer, who might win was anybody's guess. The candidates' relative strengths and weaknesses seemed to be of equal significance, and Democrats across the city – sometimes even members of the same family – were deeply divided.

Cannavino's nephew Skip – who was deputy city treasurer at the time – was part of one such family.

"Naturally, the position that I was in [with the city], a lot of people would ask me who I was voting for and I tried to play it as straight as can be," Skip said. "I would tell them 'I'm voting for my uncle.'"[16]

Skip's father was Mike Cannavino's brother.

Skip's mother was Lou Tullio's sister.[17]

▰ ▰ ▰

Tullio's daughter June still remembers the words her mother Ceil told her on Municipal Primary Election Night, Tuesday, May 18, 1965. On the second floor of Lou's State Street campaign headquarters, June and her parents prepared to descend the stairs and make a concession statement to supporters and media who'd gathered there.[18]

"You walk down those steps," Ceil told June. "You hold your head up high."

June, Ceil, and Lou had every right to hold their heads up high. Tullio was able to carry his home ward – the fifth, where more voters resided than anywhere else – by more than 500 votes.[19]

But it wasn't enough to propel him to victory.

Cannavino won East Side Polish wards, the first and the second, by more than 300 and 600 votes, respectively. He triumphed by less than 200 votes each in his own West Side Italian wards, the third and sixth. And he narrowly edged Tullio by just 34 votes in the Republican Fourth

---

[16] Cannavino, Skip. Author interview with Skip Cannavino. 8 Jan 2015.

[17] Ibid.

[18] Pintea, June. Author interview with June Pintea. 22 Jan. 2015.

[19] Garvey, William P. PhD. *The Ethnic Factor in Erie Politics.* PhD. diss, University of Pittsburgh, 1973.

Ward.[20]

Tullio – a political neophyte – had come incredibly close to defeating an experienced and powerful career politician; he lost by a total of 915 votes – 14,486 to 13,571 – or less than two percent.[21]

Mayor Williamson must have been pleased by this outcome; without a primary opponent of his own, the Republican expended neither words nor cash as he watched the two Italian Democrats attack each other throughout the spring of 1965. Moreover, Williamson had commissioned a private poll that suggested he could beat Cannavino, but not Tullio.[22]

Both Williamson and Cannavino thought themselves in an enviable position heading in to the November general election.

Williamson's tenure as mayor was wrought with partisan obstructionism brought on by growing pains from the new strong mayor form of government; the perceived lack of action on Williamson's part – especially in regards to roads, streets, parking, and traffic issues – angered voters.

He blamed the majority-Democrat council, and by association, Cannavino.

Cannavino – who just four years prior had covertly backed Williamson over fellow Democrat and incumbent Mayor Art Gardner – claimed that he'd attempted cooperation in the past, without success.[23]

As Williamson went about his work painting Cannavino as a saboteur, Cannavino – who may have been intellectually outclassed by the University of Chicago-educated[24] educator Williamson – campaigned just as he'd always done, holding rallies, making appearances at social clubs, and otherwise adhering to the same rigorous schedule he'd followed prior to his heart attack.

A week prior to his death, Cannavino was greeting supporters at the Calabrese Club, an important cultural and political gathering place in Little Italy. His nephew Skip remembers thinking that he "didn't look good," and was worried that others noticed, too.[25]

Then on Friday, October 22, Mike Cannavino attended a rally at the Knights of St. John social club. A witness in attendance, Leona Bog-

---

[20] Ibid.

[21] Ibid.

[22] Foust, Kyle. "Why Lou Tullio: How Erie's Most Powerful Mayor Came to Power." Journal of Erie Studies 32, no. 2, 2003: 57-75.

[23] Ibid.

[24] Garvey, William P. PhD. The Ethnic Factor in Erie Politics. PhD. diss, University of Pittsburgh, 1973.

[25] Cannavino, Skip. Author interview with Skip Cannavino. 8 Jan 2015.

danski, reported that Cannavino – fatigued, pale, and nearly unintelligible – looked as though he may not have much longer to live.[26]

She was right.

Cannavino, who had recently taken up residence at the Lawrence Hotel[27] on the corner of 10th and State Streets strictly for the convenience of it, retired to room 305 late that same evening. The next day, after failing to respond to phone calls and worried knocks upon his door, he was found around 1 p.m. by his campaign manager, dead in his bed.[28]

✦ ✦ ✦

At 4 p.m. on that blustery Sunday of October 24, 1965, Erie County Democratic Party Chair Robert Horn convened the special meeting of committee members charged with choosing Cannavino's replacement on the ballot.

But as those 144 committee members – two from each of the 72 districts that made up the city's six wards – took their seats, many of them didn't know that the outcome of that meeting was a foregone conclusion.

Upon Cannavino's death, Tullio wasn't the only one who fancied taking his place on the ballot. Several elected officials, including City Councilmen Robert Glowacki, Joseph Robie, and Richard Scheffner, as well as City Controller candidate Arthur Gehrlein were mentioned as also being interested.[29] Cannavino supporters pushed for his close friend Julian Polaski, or his campaign manager, Jack Fatica – both of whom could resurrect their expectations of benefitting from the patronage jobs that would result from victory.

And then, of course, there was Tullio.

To sort out the hodge-podge of aspirants, a series of closed-door meetings between the Tullio and Cannavino organizations had begun on Saturday night.[30] Democrats thought it essential that they emerge from this tragedy united, lest they leave Mayor Williamson with yet another opportunity to steal the mayoralty.

Cannavino's people, still smarting from their sudden loss, were un-

---

[26] Foust, Kyle. "Why Lou Tullio: How Erie's Most Powerful Mayor Came to Power." *Journal of Erie Studies* 32 no. 2, 2003: 57-75.

[27] Cannavino, Skip. Author interview with Skip Cannavino. 8 Jan 2015.

[28] Ibid.

[29] Minegar, Mike. "City Mourns Mike." *Erie Times News.* 24 Oct. 1965: sec. 1, p. 1.

[30] Ibid.

wavering in their insistence that the replacement be anyone *but* Tullio, who could be perceived by the public as a "loser."[31]

Not surprisingly, it is alleged that punches were thrown at one of these meetings.

But when Tullio pulled in to his driveway early that morning only to find Erie County Democratic Party Chairman Robert Horn[32] waiting there for him, Horn told him that an agreement had been made whereby Tullio would be nominated to replace Cannavino at the meeting later that day.

During the meeting, a Third Ward Democratic Committeeman by the name of Joseph Gervase formally nominated Tullio. Fourth Ward Chairman Frank Ward seconded the nomination. No one else was nominated, Tullio was approved unanimously, and just 15 minutes after the meeting had started, it was over.[33]

* * *

The next day, Monday, was only a week and a day removed from Election Day. Mayor Williamson – out of respect for Cannavino – suspended campaign operations until after Cannavino's funeral that Wednesday at St. Paul's Roman Catholic Church.[34] It is not known if Tullio officially suspended his, however, his first public appearance wasn't until Thursday of that week, just five days before the election.

His first stop[35] as the Democratic nominee for Mayor of the City of Erie was an important one – the Calabrese Club, home to the West Side Italians he couldn't quite win over during his campaign against Cannavino.

Tullio needed more than just the support of his neighbors in the Fifth Ward. He needed the support of the Third and Sixth wards – wards that, under Cannavino's influence, had almost singlehandedly put Williamson in office four years prior. Tullio also needed to allay the suspicions of the Cannavino camp, who were still upset that one of their

---

[31] Foust, Kyle. "Why Lou Tullio: How Erie's Most Powerful Mayor Came to Power." Journal of Erie Studies, vol. 32, no. 2 (2003): 57-75.

[32] Ibid.

[33] Ibid.

[34] "Mike A. Cannavino obituary." Erie Morning News. 25 Oct. 1965: sec. B, p. 2.

[35] Foust, Kyle. "Why Lou Tullio: How Erie's Most Powerful Mayor Came to Power." Journal of Erie Studies, vol. 32, no. 2 (2003): 57-75.

own (Fatica, Polaski) hadn't been chosen to replace Cannavino.

Whatever Tullio did at the Calabrese Club that day – or behind closed doors in the days before – must have worked. Over the 5-day campaign that Tullio would go on to wage against Williamson, Fatica, Polaski, and other members of Cannavino's inner circle appeared with him publicly[36] at rallies, presenting a unified front.

"My dad ordered me, so to speak, to go on TV and represent the Cannavino family to be for Lou Tullio," Skip Cannavino said. "And that part, I had no qualms in doing that."[37]

Another olive branch was soon to be passed, this time from the Tullio camp. Part of Tullio's messaging was to invoke the memory of Cannavino; although it wasn't his main focus, Tullio portrayed himself as a man called upon to complete the earthly work of Cannavino.[38]

More practically, Tullio's messaging centered around Williamson's perceived lack of fiscal acumen; Williamson had raised taxes without addressing the most visible needs of the city – infrastructure. Tullio had experience managing a budget *larger* than the city's, and attempted to remind voters that he was more qualified to handle the city's purse strings.

Williamson shot back by defending his accomplishments[39] – namely, the construction of the Erie Zoo, and the widening of 12th Street – as well as taking moral jabs at Tullio for being at a racetrack when he learned of Cannavino's death. Astutely, Williamson also attempted to poke holes in the shaky alliance the Cannavino crew had formed with Tullio, publicly stating "you know and I know he was not and is not Mike Cannavino's choice."[40]

As Election Day dawned, local politicos called for turnout above 80 percent;[41] pleasant temperatures in the mid-50s encouraged voters to make the trip to the polls, but many questions remained. Was Tullio perceived as a benchwarmer, the second-best choice Democrats could make? Would his fragile agreement with his former opponents hold up? Would Williamson's insinuations about Tullio's character and Cannavino's wishes resonate with the people?

---

[36] Ibid.
[37] Cannavino, Skip. Author interview with Skip Cannavino. 8 Jan 2015.
[38] Foust, Kyle. "Why Lou Tullio: How Erie's Most Powerful Mayor Came to Power." Journal of Erie Studies 32 no. 2, 2003: 57-75.
[39] Ibid.
[40] Ibid.
[41] Ibid.

The answer was apparent early in the evening; Williamson conceded to Tullio before 9:30 p.m.[42] Almost 75 percent of voters made it to the polls, and almost 54 percent of them chose Tullio.[43]

Not only did Tullio again carry his home ward, the Fifth Ward, by more than 700 votes, but he also captured the rest of the East Side, winning the First Ward by almost 900 votes and the Second Ward by a stunning 2,200 votes – almost tripling Williamson's total there.[44]

On the West Side, the heavily Republican Fourth Ward went for Williamson – to no one's surprise – by more than 1,000 votes.[45]

The Third and Sixth Wards – the most crucial for Tullio – performed just well enough to add to Tullio's already-significant margins over Williamson; he took the Third Ward by more than 350 votes, and the Sixth Ward by more than 700.[46]

In total, Tullio had defeated Williamson 26,403 to 22,580.[47]

It was the narrowest margin of victory "Lucky Lou" Tullio would ever again see over his six terms as mayor, but it was a victory nonetheless, and for the first time since Ellicott had laid out the grid that would become Erie in 1795 – with all its economic, ethnic, geographical, religious, and social variation – an Italian was in charge.

---

[42] Ibid.
[43] Garvey, William P. PhD. The Ethnic Factor in Erie Politics. PhD. diss, University of Pittsburgh, 1973.
[44] Ibid.
[45] Ibid.
[46] Ibid.
[47] Ibid.

4

Lessons and Losses

I

T HAD BEEN QUITE A YEAR FOR LOU TULLIO. THROUGHOUT 1965, HE certainly imagined himself being sworn in as Erie's mayor on January 2, 1966, however, he probably never imagined the manner in which it would occur – as the last-minute replacement for the man who had defeated him during the primary election.

But mayor he now was, and despite the tendency of voters in Erie and beyond to make their selections based on the ethnopolitical and socioeconomic characteristics of the candidate, simply "being Italian" was not a reasonable blueprint for governance.

Now, Tullio had to actually *do* something.

During his campaign against Cannavino – and then against Williamson – the ideological asset that set Tullio's rhetoric apart from his rivals was his promotion of a grander view of Erie's future.

"Erie must move into the mainstream of its destiny to become a metropolitan community of major national importance with all that concept implies in creative growth, industrial development, recreational expansion, community service, and concern for the individual," he told the *Erie Daily Times* shortly after his mayoral victory in November 1965.[1] "Whether our city succeeds in its aspirations for these coming years is, to a great extent, my responsibility and that of my administration," he said in his inaugural address of January 3, 1966.[2]

Chillingly, Tullio went on to refer to issues that would continue to haunt Erie well into the 21st century. In that same address, he called for the renewal, rehabilitation, and redevelopment of the "old, but still good and solid neighborhoods" of Erie's East Side, as well as the elimination of Erie's so-called "brain drain" – the tendency of many students to earn college degrees at one of the area's three institutions of higher learning and then take them elsewhere.[3]

"We need them here," said Tullio of those graduates. "We need them to build the bridge between past mistakes and future greatness. But we cannot have them here unless all of us, in and out of government, join hands in working toward that more desirable and attractive goal – a better Erie."[4]

Tullio sought to achieve that goal by proposing an ambitious 5-year, $24-million capital improvements program[5] that would produce tangible enhancements to Erie's environment and infrastructure; its realization would leave Erie citizens with more robust services.

For decades, Erie had languished with an outdated fire alarm system, aging fire stations and equipment, 90 miles of unpaved streets[6] that lacked storm sewers, mediocre recreational facilities and parks, and unsightly boulevards that belied the beauty of her historic neighborhoods.[7] Additionally, the Erie's Water Works – designed to collect, clean, and distribute the city's greatest natural resource – was badly in need of expensive upgrades.

While such obvious upgrades in the quality of day-to-day life for Erie's residents would certainly earn Tullio amity, reaching into taxpay-

---

[1] "City's 45th Mayor." Erie Daily Times. 3 Jan. 1966.
[2] Ibid.
[3] Ibid.
[4] Ibid.
[5] Garvey, William P. PhD. The Ethnic Factor in Erie Politics. PhD. diss., University of Pittsburgh, 1973.
[6] "Tullio, Mayor Confer." Erie Daily Times. 17 Nov. 1965: sec. 1 p. 3.
[7] Garvey, William P. PhD. The Ethnic Factor in Erie Politics. PhD. diss., University of Pittsburgh, 1973.

ers' wallets to pay for these enhancements would instead earn him enmity.

Tullio's solution was to put old wine into new bottles by resurrecting a tempestuous issue that had ebbed and flowed for decades – Erie's water works, and its fiscal relationship with city government.

The Erie Water Works was created by an act of the Pennsylvania Legislature in 1867 with the mission of constructing and maintaining a system to "furnish a full supply of pure and wholesome water."[8] Three water commissioners – appointed by the Erie County Judge of the Court of Common Pleas – were furthermore directed to administer and compensate employees, as well as establish and collect usage fees. The mayor and city council issued bonds to finance the operation of the Water Works, and the revenue collected by the commissioners was to be given to the city treasurer to be used solely for retirement of those debts.

From 1867 to 1873, the city issued bonds totaling $675,000 (more than $13 million in 2014 dollars), all at 7 percent interest. The city paid the interest on the bonds in exchange for free water for city buildings as well as fire suppression; however, in 1881 the commissioners proposed that the cost of the city's free water be credited against their interest payments, with excess going towards principal on the bonds. The city, obviously, did not like the idea of starting to pay for what they'd been receiving for "free."[9]

Thus began a contentious and litigious period of relations between the water works and city government that culminated in an unsuccessful attempt to absorb the water works into city government proper by Mayor Mike Liebel in 1907.[10]

Where Mayor Mike Liebel failed, Mayor Charles Barber succeeded, and by the time Tullio took office in 1966, the Water Works had been a city bureau for 30 years.[11]

Undaunted by the somewhat quarrelsome history of the issue, Tullio revisited the concept of a water department that would again be

---

[8] Ibid.
[9] Ibid.
[10] Ibid.
[11] Ibid.

separate from the city's government; a water "authority," Tullio opined, could float $24 million in bonds, retain $4 million for future upgrades, and use the remaining $20 million to purchase the city water department. Tullio would then sink that $20 million into his capital improvements program.

He also proposed raising the city's water rates, which the *Erie Daily Times* claimed were "extraordinarily low" to the point where industrial customers were paying less than it actually cost to pump and process the water they were using.[12]

These solutions seemed simple enough, and there were a number of factors that appeared to be favorable to such an endeavor.

Tullio's predecessor, Mayor Williamson, had also recognized the need for such capital improvements in Erie; when Tullio first conferred[13] with Williamson shortly after the 1965 election, Williamson cited unpaved streets as well as deficiencies in the sewer system as major impediments to Erie's advancement.

Williamson, however, learned a hard lesson about the differences between the *theory* and the *practice* of governing during his sole term – he was a Republican facing a testy Democratic-controlled council, and he was also well-known for his refusal to "play politics" or deal in patronage. Accordingly, Williamson's capital improvements during his lone term were ultimately minor, and he paid for it at the polls.

Tullio, conversely, entered office with a city council comprised of all Democrats, and he was, by that time, an experienced "player."

He had also inherited a small city budget surplus upon taking office; the 1965 general fund budget was $8,665,224 but by the end of the year almost five percent *less* than that – or about $390,000 – had actually been spent.[14]

On the surface, the sale of the city water department by Erie's new mayor looked to be a *fait accompli*, as well as a tidal wave of creative problem solving and pragmatism upon which Tullio could coast to re-election in 1969.

But as it turns out, Lou Tullio himself was about to learn a hard lesson on the differences between the theory and the practice of governing.

---

[12] Ibid.
[13] "Tullio, Mayor Confer." Erie Daily Times. 17 Nov. 1965: sec. 1 p. 3.
[14] "City's 1965 Spending Down." Erie Times News. 9 Jan. 1966.

Claiming that Tullio was trying to circumvent council's oversight of the revenue generated from the sale of the water department and citing the fact that the city's stronger borrowing power would earn them a better interest rate on bonds, three councilmen – Bernard "Babe" Harkins, Robert "Bob" Brabender, and Pasqualino "Pat" Cappabianca – refused to go along with Tullio's idea. All three were Catholics, teachers, and Democrats from the Sixth Ward.

"I was opposed to it because if you sell it, and they [the proposed authority] can make money, why can't the city make money [by running it themselves]?" Cappabianca said. "And, it belonged to the people. He had no right to sell it. So I opposed it."[15]

Cappabianca was born the son of the Royal Italian Consul for Northwestern Pennsylvania.[16] As a child, he found everyone from illiterate farm workers to college professors sharing his family's dinner table each night, which gave him a deep respect for public service and a perspective not available to most. He went on to attend Strong Vincent High School, Gannon University, and Allegheny College, where he earned his master's degree. His brother, Italo, represented Erie in the Pennsylvania Legislature for 22 years.[17]

"[Tullio] had everybody coming down to council meetings in favor of this thing," said Cappabianca. "I'm talking about big shots. The guy who was the head of GE would come down and say, 'You gotta do this.' The Chamber of Commerce – 'You gotta do this.' Every accountant in Erie – Ernst & Ernst would come in and say, 'This is the perfect plan. You could use that money.'"[18]

Indeed, Tullio had strong support for his plan across a wide spectrum of the community. In addition to General Electric and the Chamber of Commerce, the *Erie Daily Times*, labor unions, and the Roman Catholic Diocese also supported Tullio.[19]

Augmenting that support, Tullio had other important tools to work with in pushing his plan; although he was an educated man, his life experiences in sports, in the military, and in politics taught him valuable life

---

[15] Cappabianca, Pat. Author interview with Pat Cappabianca. 5 Jan. 2015
[16] Green, Cornell. "You Ought to Know: Pat Cappabianca." The Erie Reader, 2 Dec. 2011.
[17] Cappabianca, Pat. Author interview with Pat Cappabianca. 5 Jan. 2015
[18] Ibid.
[19] Garvey, William P. PhD. The Ethnic Factor in Erie Politics. PhD. diss., University of Pittsburgh, 1973.

lessons – lessons on how to how to connect with people, and on how to lead from the front. As a result, Tullio was a shrewd evaluator of talent and an effective mediator of interpersonal disputes. These traits – plus a solid work ethic – would serve him well in his staffing decisions and in his handling of constituents, both during his first term, and beyond.

One of the first people Tullio hired upon his election to mayor was his old friend, Pat Liebel. During the race, Tullio asked the highly-capable and well-qualified Liebel if she would accompany him to City Hall in the event that he defeated Williamson.[20]

"Absolutely not!" Liebel said.

When Tullio asked her why, she reminded him that she had built up some seniority – and a pension[21] – over the years she'd worked with him and his predecessor Art Logan at the Erie School District.

"So he said, 'Well, think about it,' and I guess he asked me every day, you know, did I decide? Did I decide? And I told him 'no' up until the last minute," said Liebel.[22]

It was a fortuitous change of heart for Liebel, who was indispensable to – and nearly synonymous with – Tullio for the rest of his political career. Their collective political fates thus intertwined, Tullio and Liebel would together experience great triumph, disappointing loss, and befuddling treachery, as well as more than a few groundbreaking firsts.

"He always kidded me," she said, "the biggest decision I ever made was to walk across State Street."[23] In those days, the offices of the Erie School District were in the offices of the old library at Seventh and French streets, just across State Street from the municipal building at Sixth and State.

Another early ally who *didn't* have to cross the street was Joe Robie. Although Robie (who was Polish) shared several characteristics with Tullio's first-term agitators Brabender, Cappabianca, and Harkins – he was Catholic, and a teacher, a Democrat, and from the Sixth Ward – Robie, who played right guard on the Tullio-coached Erie Vets semi-pro football team in 1948,[24] resigned from city council in 1966 to become Tullio's administrative assistant.[25]

---

[20] Liebel, Patricia. Author interview with Patricia Liebel. 7 Jan. 2015.
[21] Ibid.
[22] Ibid.
[23] Ibid.
[24] Lyon, Debbi. Coach Lou Tullio and Erie Vets 1948 Football at Erie Stadium. 11 Jul. 2012. 9 Mar. 2015.
[25] Flowers, Kevin. Longtime City Leader Robie Dies at 82. 8 July 2006. Erie Times News. Accessed 14 Mar. 2015.

With Liebel and Robie on board, Tullio's talent for evaluating people was apparent and completely aligned with his essentially blue-collar personality.

Tullio was very much a real Erie guy. He liked to cook.[26] He liked to eat. He struggled with his weight.[27] He hung out at the track.[28] He was an avid golfer. He played handball.[29] He liked to make and drink Manhattans (sparingly), and enjoyed a cigar on occasion.[30] He wasn't overly materialistic,[31] cared little for fancy cars,[32] and sometimes kept defective furnishings in his home.[33] But he answered his city hall phone personally, as much as he could, and kept his home phone listed in the phone book the entire time he was mayor.[34]

And he'd answer that phone, too; the stories about the phone calls he'd receive at home have become the stuff of local legend.

"One time, a guy called him up about 3 o'clock in the morning, and he [the caller] was really, really upset," Liebel said.[35] The caller's garbage hadn't been picked up because, as Tullio soon learned, the caller had called the garbage collector "a dumb Pollack."[36]

He told the caller that he shouldn't have slurred the garbage collector, and that he wouldn't have picked up the caller's garbage *either*.

He also told the caller that his garbage would be picked up the next morning anyway.

Tullio then phoned the director of public works and told him that if he couldn't find someone to pick up the irate caller's garbage the next day – schedule be damned – then he (the director) was to pick it up himself.[37]

"The next night," said Liebel, "the very next night, at 3 o'clock in the morning, Lou calls the guy back… and asked him if his garbage had been picked up. I don't think the guy ever called again."[38]

---

[26] McKean, Edwin. Author interview with Edwin McKean. 23 Jan. 2015.

[27] Pintea, June. Author interview with June Pintea. 22 Jan. 2015.

[28] Liebel, Patricia. Author interview with Patricia Liebel. 7 Jan. 2015.

[29] Ibid.

[30] Pintea, June. Author interview with June Pintea. 22 Jan. 2015.

[31] McKean, Edwin. Author interview with Edwin McKean. 23 Jan. 2015.

[32] Ibid.

[33] Ibid

[34] Liebel, Patricia. Author interview with Patricia Liebel. 7 Jan. 2015.

[35] Ibid.

[36] Ostrowski, Mark. "The Beginning of a Regime: An Analysis of Louis J. Tullio's Governing Style, 1961 - 1969." 1991.

[37] Ibid.

[38] Liebel, Patricia. Author interview with Patricia Liebel. 7 Jan. 2015.

Tullio had a particular way of handling people that could best be described as a sincere-yet-erudite simplicity. When he spoke, people listened; occasionally, they then wondered what, exactly, they'd just heard.

"He used to make such malapropisms," said Cappabianca in hindsight, "that I would hit the guy next to me and say 'Did you understand what he said?' Because he just rambled on and sometimes you couldn't understand him... he sounded like a big dummy. Terrible. He had no command as a speaker. Well, I find out years later, the guy's brilliant."

Verbal gaffes aside, Tullio's simple style was effective and endearing to many. But to back up his oral promises, he worked persistently and assiduously.

"He was a morning person, but he was there all day," said Liebel. "If he had to meet with somebody at five or six o'clock he stayed until five or six o'clock after being there [all day]. But he was always in the office by at least 8:00 [a.m.] and he'd just start in as soon as he got there."

It got to the point that everyone, in every department, did the same despite their mandated 8:30 start because they figured he'd be in, and he'd probably be looking for them.[39]

Around noon, Tullio would visit the Erie Downtown YMCA, which was a notorious political hangout and also where, coincidentally, Skip Cannavino first learned of his uncle Mike Cannavino's death in the hotel across the street.[40] Like Skip, Tullio would play handball, chew the political fat, and return to his city job around 1:15 in the afternoon.

"I mean, he never stopped going," Liebel said of Tullio. "And then in the evening he had activities constantly, and he went to every wedding he was invited to."[41]

Liebel underscored her point by saying that he would sometimes hand her five or six wedding invitations at a time.

"Put these on my calendar," he'd say.

"You can't go to all these weddings," she'd say. "They're all on the same day!"

Once, Liebel says, he went to three weddings on the same day. "He said, 'Well, you're invited, you got to go!' And I thought, you know, that was him – he never slowed down."[42]

---

[39] Ibid.
[40] Cannavino, Skip. Author interview with Skip Cannavino. 8 Jan. 2015.
[41] Liebel, Patricia. Author interview with Patricia Liebel. 7 Jan. 2015.
[42] Ibid.

Of course, there were reasons Tullio adhered to such a taxing schedule; aside from his genuine interest in his friends, his neighbors, and his constituents, the old joke goes that when Tullio attends a wedding on a Saturday, there are two new hires in the streets department come Monday.

Despite his staff, his style, and his support – the kind of support he earned with his busy schedule and vigilant responsiveness to constituent issues – he still needed 5 votes on city council to sell the water authority. All Cappabianca, Harkins, or Brabender had to do was roll with the tide and let their fellow Democrat Tullio have some leeway, and they in turn would have had a far easier time charting their own respective political courses.

However, their refusal to change their tack on an issue they all felt strongly about taught Tullio (and Erie itself) that mayor-council conflict would be a permanent fixture of the post-1961 strong mayor form of government, regardless of party affiliation, ethnicity, or religion. Tullio only had four votes; Brabender, Harkins, and Cappabianca withstood withering pressure, and sank Tullio's plan in April 1967. They in turn presented their own leaner counterproposal,[43] which – rather than an outright sale – suggested leasing the water works to an authority, and then using the lease income to finance capital improvements. Tullio proclaimed the plan "insufficient," had the votes to defeat it, and did so in May.[44]

▰ ▰ ▰

That summer of 1967 was a watershed of sorts; great cultural, political, and social change was taking place across the globe, across the country, and across Erie.

In the mid-1950s, African-Americans were an ethnic minority in Erie that was only just beginning to take advantage of their socioeconomic maturation; their main problem, however, lie in their overall numbers, as their population was still negligible in relation to white ethnic groups, electorally speaking.[45]

But after years of segregation, criminalization, discrimination, and

---

[43] Cappabianca, Pat. Author interview with Pat Cappabianca. 5 Jan. 2015.
[44] Garvey, William P. PhD. The Ethnic Factor in Erie Politics. PhD. diss., University of Pittsburgh, 1973.
[45] Ibid.

marginalization, the grievous plight and the growing power of African-Americans was becoming harder and harder to ignore.

Tullio related well[46] with African-Americans on a personal level; his experience as a sportsman, a coach, and a member of a still-segregated-yet-integrating United States Military put him in regular contact with this oft-insular community at a time when interracial interaction was relatively limited both by custom and, in some parts of the country, by law.

Furthermore, President Kennedy's "New Frontier" initiative to strengthen civil rights in the early 1960s and President Johnson's "Great Society" initiative to reduce urban poverty and discrimination in 1964 and 1965 had convinced African-Americans by-and-large that the Democratic Party was now the only party worth supporting.

The cumulative result of Tullio's racial perspective and the Democratic Party's relative appeal was that during his contest with Williamson in 1965, Tullio won African-American districts in the Second and Fifth Wards by substantial margins.[47]

By 1967, African-Americans across the country and in Erie still felt that their issues fell on mostly-deaf ears, despite their newly-formidable presence in the political arena. Contributing to their disenchantment was the escalation of the Vietnam War, which had seen troop levels spike dramatically from just 900 in 1960 to more than 536,000 in 1968.[48] The draft associated with the increasingly-unpopular Vietnam War compelled African-Americans to fight for a country that barely recognized their own civil rights.

To complicate matters further, the November 1963 assassination of President Kennedy and the February 1965 assassination of Malcom X only added to pre-existing racial tension, leading to race riots in 1967 that occurred from Atlanta to Boston to Buffalo to Tampa, and from Minneapolis to Milwaukee to Chicago to New York in what would become known as the "long hot summer."

A bi-partisan commission created by President Johnson and headed by Illinois Governor Otto Kerner, Jr. issued a report attempting, among

---

[46] Rush, Fred. Author interview with Fred Rush. 13 Jan. 2015.
[47] Garvey, William P. PhD. The Ethnic Factor in Erie Politics. PhD. diss., University of Pittsburgh, 1973.
[48] Ostrowski, Mark. "The Beginning of a Regime: An Analysis of Louis J. Tullio's Governing Style, 1961 - 1969." 1991.

other things, to identify the root causes of the riots; the commission's findings – published on February 29, 1968 as the *Report of the National Advisory Commission on Civil Disorders* but known popularly as the *Kerner Report* – stated that unequal access to economic opportunity was to blame.[49]

The Kerner Commission's findings didn't vary much from Tullio's inauguration-day goals of remaking Erie as an enviable, affordable place to live, learn, work, play, and conduct business.

Accordingly, April 4, 1968 found Tullio in Washington, D.C., searching for other ways to finance Erie's rejuvenation after his nose-bloodying over the water authority.[50] On this day, he sought federal funds to help the Hammermill Paper Company[51] find alternatives to dumping their wastewater into Lake Erie. But when word of Martin Luther King's assassination on a balcony outside room 306 of the Lorraine Motel in Memphis at 6:01 p.m. that evening reached him, he returned home to Erie as quickly as possible.

Rioting broke out in many cities, including Erie, and according to longtime Tullio aide Fred Rush,[52] Tullio dove into the epicenter near 18th and Holland Streets, got up on the back of a truck, grabbed a microphone, and delivered another now-famous "Tullio-ism" that helped calm tensions.

"He came up with the police chief, and grabbed a microphone, got on the back of a truck and said, 'You guys can't do this!'" Rush said. "'You're hurting the neighborhood and hurting the city!'"

Trying to reach protesters the best way he knew how, Tullio cited his familiarity with Erie's African-American community.

"I know most of y'all! I coached some of you guys! Willy! And Aaron!" Tullio said, singling out members of the crowd with whom he was acquainted.

As the crowd hushed, Tullio continued.

"You know I'm a straight shooter, honest to God I'm right on top of it, and you know I'll call a spade a spade!"

---

[49] National Advisory Commission on Civil Disorders. "Report of the National Advisory Commission on Civil Disorders." 1968.

[50] Ostrowski, Mark. "The Beginning of a Regime: An Analysis of Louis J. Tullio's Governing Style, 1961 - 1969." 1991.

[51] Ibid.

[52] Rush, Fred. Author interview with Fred Rush. 13 Jan. 2015.

The crowd fell silent.

Tullio didn't realize that the term "spade" had become a derogatory term for African-Americans.[53] What Tullio had actually meant was that he was a straight shooter – he called things as they saw them, he was nonjudgmental, and he was certainly not a racist.

"What happened? What did I say?" he asked the police chief.

"Keep talking! Keep talking!" The chief said.

Tullio's honest mistake – a Tullioism that could have been disastrous – merely served to highlight his sincerity.

A few weeks later, Tullio's water authority woes were finally resolved, although not quite to the extent that he had hoped. A watered-down plan was approved in May 1968 whereby the city itself would issue bonds to fund Tullio's ambitious capital improvements program, albeit at a level less than he'd originally proposed; the status of the city's water works was not addressed.

However, Tullio's important forays into Washington D.C. in search of federal funds would prove worthwhile throughout the rest of his career – as Johnson's "Great Society" programs began to reach the states, the amount of federal aid to cities increased from $4.9 billion in 1958 to $18.6 billion in 1968,[54] and Lou Tullio was adamant that Erie get more than its fair share.

＊ ＊ ＊

Cast amidst this backdrop of great change that thrashed and seethed both inside and outside of Erie, Lou Tullio began to consider re-election in 1969.

His handling of crises like the riots and his compromises on issues like the water authority – as well as the patronage he wielded – left him well-positioned within his own party; in the May 20, 1969 Municipal Primary Election, Tullio defeated token opposition in the form of Charles Schmitt and Joseph Lewonas, Jr. with ease, winning all six wards and taking 67 percent of the vote.[55]

---

[53] Ibid.
[54] Ostrowski, Mark. "The Beginning of a Regime: An Analysis of Louis J. Tullio's Governing Style, 1961 - 1969." 1991.
[55] Ibid.

But as Tullio was running for re-election, his wife Ceil was running out of time.

During the primary, Ceil was diagnosed with breast cancer.[56] What was not known initially is that the breast cancer was not the primary locus of the dreaded disease – Ceil had a brain tumor that had metastasized. Being a very private woman from a very private family that also included a very public man, Ceil preferred to keep her illness a secret. People around town knew that she was ill, but few – even close family members – knew the true extent of her illness.[57]

Tullio's triumphant primary victory and his wife's distressing formal diagnosis both occurred in May, leaving Lou Tullio with a delicate balancing act – he had to care for his ailing wife, and he had to run a general election campaign against an opponent who, when revealed, came as a shock to the local Democratic establishment.

Republicans – who by that time had been completely shut out of city government for four years – were in quite a quandary. Fielding a candidate of substance from their own ranks was a near impossibility, but, taking lessons from Cannavino's "defeat" of Mayor Gardner in 1961 with his wedge-like "Democratic Boosters for Williamson" organization, the local Republican organization nominated President of City Council Bob Brabender, a lifelong Democrat.

The son of a former councilman and part of a prominent Erie family with a political lineage stretching back to the 1880s,[58] Bob Brabender had been one of Tullio's city council opponents on the water issue back in 1966; he explained his party switch by citing his concern for the city while hinting at misconduct by the Tullio administration. Brabender defeated another former city councilman, Dr. Quentin Orlando, by a margin of almost 2-to-1 in a Republican primary election where the most notable and telling feature was the low voter turnout.

But the campaigns – Tullio's *and* Brabender's – were both overshadowed by Ceil's illness, as Tullio reduced his schedule to spend more time with her.

"He tried to be there," their daughter June said. "He really did try

---

[56] Pintea, June. Author interview with June Pintea. 22 Jan. 2015.

[57] Tullio, John and Norma. Author interview with John and Norma Tullio. 15 Jan. 2015.

[58] Nies III, Thomas G. *A Study of the Brabender Family and their Role in Erie Political History*. Mercyurst College. Erie, Pa., 1999.

to be there as much as he could. He did. I will say that for him – that he really really tried."[59]

At some point that summer of 1969, Ceil entered the hospital. When there wasn't much more that could be done, she returned home in September.

"The day that she came home from the hospital, he had a political rally downstairs in the basement, and I saw my mother was in the family room," said June. "There was a bay window and she was sitting in one of the chairs and it was in the early part of the afternoon. I think it was about 1:00 and she was sitting in the chair there, and she looked so peaceful. And Dad said, 'There's some people coming later, and they'd like to see you. Would you be agreeable to that?'"[60]

Erie's First Lady refused.

"So then she asked me to take her back to the bedroom, which I did – and then she never really came out after that."

Around that time, Ceil lapsed into a coma; her illness took its toll on the entire Tullio family, but June stepped up and took her mother's place in her father's increasingly vibrant political life.

"I went to different functions with my father," she said. "I think there was only one that I couldn't do it because she was very, very ill, and it was almost towards the end, and I went through all the things that a political daughter or son or whatever would go through."

As Ceil's absence was certainly notable, people would often enquire as to her condition. June put on a pleasant face.

"I'd say, 'Oh, you know not too bad. She's doing okay,'" she said, recounting one night in particular, near the end of the campaign against Brabender. "That was a tough night for me, and I remember saying 'I want to go home. I just want to go back to the house.'"

With election night fast approaching, Tullio's victory was never really in doubt. Polls[61] showed Tullio up by around 10 points during the campaign, and despite the loss of some defecting Democrats who left with Brabender, Tullio's pro-business water authority fight – as well as the dealings he'd had at the school board – helped make inroads with Republicans who mightn't've considered him prior.

---

[59] Pintea, June. Author interview with June Pintea. 22 Jan. 2015.
[60] Ibid.
[61] Garvey, William P. PhD. The Ethnic Factor in Erie Politics. PhD. diss., University of Pittsburgh, 1973.

Victory was confirmed at his election night party, when, at 9:07 p.m., an exuberant supporter referring to Brabender shouted, "He's conceded!"[62]

***

In his tree-shaded ranch-style home spread out over two lots at 660 E. Grandview Boulevard, Tullio received word of his victory while holding solemn vigil at the bedside of his wife of 28 years, who remained in a coma.[63]

"Ceil has been a better first lady than I have been a mayor," he told the *Erie Morning News* that night. "I feel the faithful citizens of Erie realize this is a very trying time and understand that my first obligation is to my wife, and this is why I chose to remain at home. The people will understand."[64]

Then, in an uncharacteristic moment for a stereotypical 1960s meat-and-potatoes Midwestern man – a man who'd spent his adolescence during the Great Depression on the oft-brutal football gridiron, and spent his young adulthood working on a dairy farm before witnessing the savagery of a global conflagration, and spent his most recent years in bare-knuckled battle with the titans of Erie politics – Lou Tullio began to weep.[65]

"I'll try to tell her," he sobbed through tears. "I'll touch her shoulder and whisper, 'We won, honey.'"[66]

Would Ceil ever know?

"I don't think so," their daughter June remarked. "No, I don't think so."[67]

Barely two days later, at 10:40 p.m. on Thursday, November 6, 1969,[68] Mary Cecelia McHale Tullio – a woman of uncommon beauty, character, courage, and wisdom according to those who best knew her – finally lost her battle with the relentless and merciless scourge of cancer. She was just 52 years old.

---

[62] Sundberg, Peggy. "Tullio's Win - Tears of Joy and Sadness." Erie Morning News. 5 Nov. 1969: sec. 1, p. 1.

[63] Sundberg, Peggy. "Brabender Concedes Early." Erie Morning News. 5 Nov. 1969: sec. 1, p.1.

[64] Ibid.

[65] Ibid.

[66] Ibid.

[67] Pintea, June. Author interview with June Pintea, 22 Jan. 2015.

[68] "Erie's First Lady Dies After Lingering Illness." Erie Morning News. 7 Nov. 1969.

5

Dear and Beloved Enemies

────────────── // ──────────────

IN NOVEMBER 1969, ERIE'S FIRST ITALIAN MAYOR – AND FIRST TRUE
"strong mayor" – was re-elected despite a first term that could be
described as a tenuous dance:

One step forward, two steps back. Two steps forward, one step
back.

Although Lou Tullio did manage to pass a meager package of capital improvements by 1968, his grandiose proposal to sell the city's water
department had gone nowhere and had consumed nearly two years of
his time and his political capital.

His once-fragmented Democratic party had united behind him and
taken all seven seats on city council, yet they obstructed his water authority and also produced his next mayoral opponent.

Tullio's margin of victory was impressive, however; he won five of
six wards with 58 percent of the vote, counting 27,373 votes to Bob
Brabender's 19,728.[1] In his East Side Polish strongholds – the First and

────────────────────────────

[1] Ostrowski, Mark. "The Beginning of a Regime: An Analysis of Louis J. Tullio's
Governing Style, 1961 - 1969." 1991.

Second Wards – he piled up a 2,600-vote advantage. In the Italian Third and Sixth Wards, that advantage was more than 2,300 votes. Brabender gained ground in the traditionally-Republican Fourth Ward, to the tune of 360 votes, but once Tullio's home ward – the Fifth Ward – was counted, his total lead jumped from around 4500 votes to more than 7600.

During this election, the results from two wards in particular demonstrate important keys to Tullio's victory.

In the Fourth Ward, Brabender – who had been a Republican for all of six months – failed to completely court Erie's West Side lakefront blue-bloods, and only prevailed 2,734 to 2,374. Mayor Williamson, by contrast, was a dyed-in-the-wool Republican and beat Tullio in the same ward in 1965 by more than a thousand votes. Some of Tullio's success in the Fourth Ward during the election of 1969 can probably be attributed to the credibility he'd earned with Erie's business community over his capital improvements program, but it wasn't quite enough; Brabender won the Fourth Ward anyway, and in doing so would become the last "Republican" candidate for mayor to take an entire city ward, through the mayoral elections of 2013.

The Fifth Ward – where Tullio resided, albeit no longer in the family "compound" on 25th and Brandes streets[2] but in a new house he'd built near Mercyhurst Preparatory High School – was a good place to be from; the Fifth Ward always showed up strong for Tullio, dating back to his primary loss to Cannavino.

More importantly, 15,452 people voted in the Fifth Ward, as compared to 5,142 in the First Ward, 4,072 in the Second Ward, 4,554 in the Third Ward, and 5,108 in the Fourth Ward.[3] The 2,954-vote advantage Tullio picked up in the fifth meant that even if Brabender had reproduced Williamson's 1,000-vote trouncing in the Fourth Ward, and won the First Ward, the Second Ward, and his own home ward – the Sixth Ward – by slim margins, he *still* would have lost to Tullio. The Fifth Ward made Tullio mayor in 1965, and on Tuesday, November 4, 1969, it would help keep him mayor.

Although Tullio had just posted another convincing electoral victory, it was bittersweet.

---

[2] Pintea, June. Author interview with June Pintea. 22 Jan. 2015.
[3] Ostrowski, Mark. "The Beginning of a Regime: An Analysis of Louis J. Tullio's Governing Style, 1961 - 1969." 1991.

"I wish I could say that this was the happiest day of my life," Tullio would go on to state,[4] but the loss of his wife of almost 30 years gave him little cause for celebration.

"I thought he did pretty well," said daughter June, of her father's emotional state after the passing of her mother, Ceil. "In some ways, you're happy that she's at peace, and I think that he was. He felt that sense of letting go."

The loss of his wife was certainly a step back for him personally. However, as humankind was for the first time setting foot on the moon, Erie was also taking one small step towards the "metropolitan community of major national importance" that Tullio had referred to shortly after his 1965 election.[5] Tullio himself had taken another step forward by posting a convincing electoral victory. Halting progress was being made, and because Tullio had claimed responsibility for the success or failure of his administration's goals, he had to keep taking steps forward.

And although he may not have known it at the time, Tullio had already taken the most important step forward of any mayor – before, or since.   ✦ ✦ ✦

In yet another coincidence for "Lucky Lou" Tullio, he happened to be mayor of Erie at probably the most opportune time – before or since.

"When he was mayor, it was the good times," said Fred Rush.[6]

Rush was born in 1943 and migrated to Erie from Mississippi with his parents in 1946. Like many African-Americans of the time, Rush's parents sought economic opportunity and a fair education for their children in a pre-*Brown v. Board of Education* United States where "separate but equal" was certainly separate but certainly not equal.

Unlike many African-Americans of the time, Rush's parents were college-educated; as such, they wanted their own children to follow in those footsteps.

"You're lucky you only have four letters in your last name!" Rush's mother said to him when he was a young child.

"Why?"

"I expect more letters *after* your name than *in* your name," she told

---

[4] Sundberg, Peggy. "Brabender Concedes Early." Erie Morning New.s 5 Nov. 1969: sec. 1, p.1.
[5] "City's 45th Mayor." Erie Daily Times. 3 Jan. 1966.
[6] Rush, Fred. Author interview with Fred Rush. 13 January 2015.

him. "Get your bachelor's, get your master's."

Such were the expectations in the Rush family.[7] His older sister has a Bachelor of Arts and an Master of Fine Arts from Mercyhurst University; his middle sister has a bachelor's degree from Mount Holyoke College and Bachelor of Science in Nursing from Villa Maria, as well as a Doctor of Divinity from Paine Theological Seminary; his youngest sister – one of only 40 Fulbright Scholarship recipients each year – has two degrees from Gannon University, plus one from Mercyhurst.[8]

After a stint at Penn State University Park as well as a stint in Vietnam, Rush earned his Bachelor's Degree in Sociology and Political Science from Gannon University, and was working there in 1969 when a strange turn of events led to him joining the Tullio administration.

"I saw this newspaper article, it said something like, 'Black Man Rapes White Woman,' – that kind of thing – and it made me angry. So I take it down to the newspaper, there's two guys in charge – I didn't know them."

He walked in, threw the paper down, and said, "This is derogatory and inflammatory! And poorly written."

"Who the hell are you?" the guys in charge said.

"I'm working at Gannon, going back to school in a little bit," said Rush.

The bigger of the two guys stood up and said, "Hey, you want to learn the newspaper business? Come to work here!"

"I don't want to work here," Rush said. "I just want to get this straightened out."

"You either work here, or you get your ass out of here!"

He didn't know it at the time,[9] but the big guy was Ed Mead – an Erie publishing giant who joined the family business as a third-generation newspaperman in 1952 and would go on to serve as co-publisher, president, editor, and author of more than 14,000 columns over a 63-year career that ended with his death in 2015.[10]

As a novice newsman, Rush's first beats with *Times Publishing* became obituaries and weather because they were, as he put it, the most

---

[7] Ibid.
[8] Ibid.
[9] Ibid.
[10] Cuneo, Kevin. "Ed Mead, Erie newspaper icon dies at 88." Erie Times News. 12 Mar. 2015.

dangerous.[11]

"You put a 'y' instead of an 'i' on a Polish name, or if you put down that the weather's going to be sunny tomorrow, and it rains like hell…" he laughed.

Rush also covered municipal government meetings across Erie County, and ultimately found himself catching the attention of Tullio.

"Lou pulled me aside one day after the time of the riots, and he said 'Do you want to keep working out there, or do you want to come inside and make a change?'"

Tullio's insightful statement on the power relationship between the 'reporter' and the 'reported on' was clear to Rush; he would go on to serve in two different periods with Tullio, but his first assignment was in the Model Cities Program office.

The Model Cities Program was one of the components of President Johnson's "War on Poverty" that lasted from 1966 until 1974.[12] With the stated aim of combating inner-city poverty, the Model Cities Program a designated an area within the city of Erie – from 12th to 26th streets, and from East Avenue to Cranberry Street – for residential redevelopment by making loans and grants to homeowners for improvements and repairs.

It was one of the most progressive public policies of the 20th century, and was also one of the reasons "Lucky Lou" was lucky to be mayor during its existence. From 1965 to 1970, federal aid to cities more than doubled, from $11.9 billion to $25 billion.[13]

"[Tullio] had one real advantage," Rush said, of the "good times" he alluded to. "When he was mayor and the Great Society programs [of which the War on Poverty was a part] started kicking in, we had money. We did hotels and motels, roads, built senior citizen centers, and all that kind of stuff. Plus, he knew enough to play the political game."

That political game, however, was played on a different field than Erie was used to playing on; during the Williamson administration – and prior – Erie was somewhat insular, financially. Formal channels to state and federal monies were nearly non-existent.[14]

---

[11] Rush, Fred. Author interview with Fred Rush. 13 January 2015.
[12] Hunt, D. Bradford. Encyclopedia of Chicago. 2005. Retrieved 31 Jan. 2015.
[13] Ostrowski, Mark. "The Beginning of a Regime: An Analysis of Louis J. Tullio's Governing Style, 1961 - 1969." 1991.
[14] Ibid.

However, this old game on a new field was played much in the same way as local patronage politics – whereas the strong mayor form of government had consolidated local clout, money, and power at the mayoral level, the rapid expansion of federal expenditures had consolidated *that* clout, money, and power at the state and federal level.

The most important step Tullio ever took was onto that field – to play in that arena.

"Lou had connections everywhere – state, federal level," said John Horan, who started off in the Erie Redevelopment Office under Tullio in 1968. "He had a lot of contacts all over the country, and he worked those contacts. So from a city the size of Erie, he performed his magic in a much larger arena than just Erie."[15]

Horan – a St. Louis, Missouri native born in 1942 – graduated from St. Benedict's College in Atchison, Kansas and earned his Master's Degree in Planning and Public Policy from Southern Illinois University Edwardsville. Upon graduation, he began to look for a job in his field.

"I came here [to Erie] for an interview," he said. "Among other things, I was shown Lake Erie, which I had never seen before – I had never seen a body of water I couldn't throw a rock across, being from the Midwest."

He got the job with the redevelopment authority, where he served until Tullio appointed him city director of policy, planning, and management in 1972. In February 1977, he began work as the executive director of the Housing Authority of the City of Erie, where he remained as of 2015.

During his time working under Tullio, Horan saw firsthand the results of Tullio's persistent lobbying.

Erie – due largely to Tullio's productive working relationship with President Richard Nixon – became one of the first 16 Model Cities in 1971, and received almost $15 million from the program through 1972.[16]

"One of his fortés was getting money from the federal government for programs," said Horan. "The Model Cities Program started in the late-60s early-70s, so we were probably getting a couple million dollars a year" during a time when the annual city budget was around $13 million.

---

[15] Horan, John. Author Interview with John Horan. 14 April 2015.
[16] Tullio, Lou. "Many Projects Planned for City." *Erie Times News*. 23 Jan. 1972: V 2.

"The Little Italy work started in the Tullio administration," Horan said. "The areas around Saint Stan's started during the Tullio administration. The whole neighborhood around 18th and Holland started in the Tullio administration. These are all fairly decent neighborhoods today, because of the groundwork that was laid back in the Model City years in the early 70s."

As 1969 drew to a close, Tullio's relationships in the federal government would become increasingly important. Warnings about the city budget being in the red surfaced as early as November,[17] and in August 1970 it was revealed that of the city's $13.3 million budget, only $5.7 million remained[18] – an uncomfortably close margin.

One of the reasons for the city's budget shortfall that was probably apparent to many Erieites and had been predicted by the Kerner Report in 1968, was that white, wealthier Americans were fleeing the nation's troubled inner cities.[19]

Suburbanization was in full swing, and Erie's largest suburb, Millcreek Township, was in the midst of explosive growth. Beginning in the 1950s, new home construction in Millcreek – where taxes, crime, and poverty were low enough to entice city-dwellers to settle there – doubled from previous decades. In the 1940s, 1,873 new houses were built in Millcreek Township, but in the 1950s, 1960s, 1970s, and 1980s, an average of 3,684 homes were built each decade.[20] Consequently, Millcreek ballooned from just 17,037 residents in 1950 to 52,129 in 2000.[21]

This growth was readily observable for most Erieites; unfortunately, this growth concealed a population shrinkage within the city itself that was not as easy to spot.

The 1970 U.S. Census was the *first ever* to record a negative growth rate for the City of Erie, dating back to 1800. Erie had posted double-digit growth from the 1880s through the 1930s; after falling flat during the Great Depression, Erie grew by almost 12 percent during the war economy of the 1940s, and by 5.7 percent in the postwar-boom

---

[17] "Tullio Discloses City Could End Year in Red." Erie Times News. 9 Nov. 1969: IIIG.

[18] "City Spent $7.6 Million in 7 Months." Erie Times News. 14 Aug. 1970: IIIG 144.

[19] National Advisory Commission on Civil Disorders. "Report of the National Advisory Commission on Civil Disorders." 1968.

[20] City-data.com. http://www.City-Data.com. n.d. 13 Feb. 2015. <http://www.city-data.com/township/Millcreek-Erie-PA.html>.

[21] Graney, Grossman, Colosimo and Associates Inc. Erie County Demographic Study. Erie County, Pa., Jan. 2003.

1950s, peaking at an all-time population high of 138,440 in the 1960 census. The 1970 census, however, showed 9,209 fewer residents, a 6.7 percent loss.[22] Regardless of the reasons, what this meant for Tullio and the city of Erie was fewer homeowners, and fewer taxpayers.

Tullio attacked this problem by again advancing a $32 million proposal that involved the sale of the city water works; he cautioned council that were it not passed, water rates would have to more than double, and property taxes would see an 8-mill increase from the then-current 15.5 mills. [23]

That proposal was again scuttled by council on December 16, with the stalwarts Cappabianca and Harkins now joined in their opposition by Dr. Quentin Orlando.[24]

Pennsylvania law demands cities pass a balanced budget by December 31 each year, and with the city's proposed 1971 budget of $15.3 million facing a $2.6 million deficit, the Tullio administration had a major problem.

But on December 27, 1970, by a 5-2 vote, council finally approved the sale of the water works. "It was just me and Harkins left," said Cappabianca; Brabender was no longer on city council. "[Tullio] has his 5 votes, and they passed it. They created the authority and they passed the sale."[25]

The seven-member water authority was to issue $32 million in bonds over 30 years, retain $4.4 million for improvements, and pay the city $27 million, from which the earned interest would help balance the city's 1971 budget with only a 1.5 mill property tax increase.

Despite the vote, however, Tullio's Christmas gift was about to be taken away.

"A citizen came in with a petition of a hundred signatures, and they wanted to put it on the ballot," Cappabianca said.

More signatures – 9,900 more, to be exact – were needed to place the question on the ballot, and gathering these signatures was no easy task; signatories had to be registered voters living in the City of Erie,

[22] United States Census Bureau. Ninteenth U.S. Census. Washington: GPO, 1970.
[23] "City Spending Borrowed Money." Erie Times News. 5 Sept. 1970: IIIG 152.
[24] Kermisch, Amos. "City Council Defeats, 4-3, Water Works Transfer." Erie Daily Times. 16 Dec. 1970: A-1.
[25] Cappabianca, Pat. Author interview with Pat Cappabianca. 5 Jan. 2015.

and could only sign the petitions at the city clerk's office.

To eliminate the burden of a trip downtown, council was asked to open the firehouses so people could sign petitions in their own neighborhoods; naturally, city council refused.[26]

This refusal made Cappabianca so angry that, that during a council meeting, he stood up from his chair, and in a move of great symbolism, walked down onto the floor – where citizens are normally heard – and said that *he* would lead the charge to get the required signatures.[27]

"We only had ten days to get 10,000 signatures, and the clerk's office had to stay open from 8 [a.m.] to 10 [p.m.] or something like that, and then they would close, right away, at 10," said Cappabianca. "And every day, the newspaper would put in there how many signatures we needed, and so on, impossible task, and so forth, and, the last night or so – I can't remember the figures, but I think we needed 2,000 signatures that night, the last night."

Erie, around Christmas time, is often an icy mess – and it certainly was on that day; it was difficult to walk, and the deadline for the signatures was rapidly approaching. Cappabianca was given 5 minutes live on WSEE-TV, which was located on 12th and Peach streets, not far from the clerk's office at Sixth and State.

He made his final appeal, and was shocked at the result. "By the time we got back to city hall, the place was jammed," he said.

That night, the last night, Cappabianca had achieved his goal of collecting the right amount of signatures to get the water works sale on the ballot. Tullio went on to challenge the validity of the petition's signatures in court. The signatures were valid, the measure went on the ballot, and the sale of the Water Works was defeated by a margin of 5-to-1.[28]

"So we were enemies, Lou Tullio and I," said Cappabianca.

---

[26] Ibid.
[27] Ibid.
[28] "Voters Reject Water Department Plan, Walczak, Orlando Lead Council Tickets." Erie Morning News. 18 May 1971: 1.

■ ■ ■

The new year of 1971 brought with it austerity; Tullio halted pay raises and made round after round of job cuts within city departments, eliminating 160 jobs by summer of 1971 while still facing a $1.1 million shortfall[29] on a budget of $13.2 million.[30] Without further action, the city would be out of money by October.

In August, property owners were warned of a potentially catastrophic increase in property taxes,[31] from what was then 17 mills to somewhere between 28 and 31 mills.

Luckily for Tullio, 11th-hour federal aid from the Nixon administration averted what could have amounted to a doubling of property taxes for Erie property owners from 1969 to 1971.[32] In the end, the city's 1972 budget – trimmed to $12.7 million from 1971's $13.3 million – was passed with only a 1 mill property tax increase,[33] a minor victory for Tullio.

But Erie's population loss in the late 1960s would mark the beginning of a trend that would continue through at least 2015; the 1970 census was the first of four consecutive censuses that would show steadily shrinking population and a rapidly-eroding tax base. From its high point in the 1960s, Erie's population had dropped from 138,000 to just less than 100,000 by mid-2015 – nearly a 30 percent loss.

Content neither to rely on the fickle nature of unsustainable federal aid injections augmenting his budgets nor to simply manage the decline of a once-bustling urban manufacturing center, Tullio needed to do something that would draw people back to the city's downtown shopping and business district centered on State Street.

His unique attraction would come to be known as the Transitway Mall.

Just after his re-election, in November 1969, Tullio suggested that State Street from Sixth to 10th Street be closed to vehicular traffic and transformed into a $1.4 million pedestrian mall. He cited Minneapolis,

[29] "$1 Million Deficit Looms for City." Erie Times News. 7 July 1971: IV-I 105.
[30] "City Spending Up A Bit, Despite Austerity Plan." Erie Morning News. 28 Jun. 1971: B-1.
[31] "11-14 Mill Tax Increas Faces Property Owners." Erie Times News. 23 Aug. 1971: IV-I 123.
[32] "Federal Aid Helped Limit Possible Tax Hike In City." Erie Morning News. 26 Nov. 1971: C-5.
[33] "Council Celebrate Eve with One Mill Tax Increase." Erie Times News. 1 Jan. 1972: IV-I 192.

Minnesota as a shining example of a dilapidated, deteriorating down-town reinvigorated by just such a feature, and brought speakers from Minneapolis to Erie to speak on the subject.[34]

By April 1970, council had approved an initial study of the Tran-sitway plan,[35] which was opposed by some downtown business owners until it finally passed council in March 1972.

In June of that year a lawsuit ensued, brought by a group called the Concerned Businessmen and headed by downtown merchant Sam Sherman, then-owner of the oldest business in Erie – Isaac Baker, a re-tail clothing store founded in 1850. Joined with Sherman in the lawsuit were owners of the Erie Sports Store, Darling Jewelry, D & K Stores, and the G.C. Murphy Company,[36] all of whom feared that forcing cus-tomers to park blocks away and walk to their State Street businesses – especially in winter – would prove disastrous.

That lawsuit was dismissed in June 1973; but just as Tullio's down-town desires seemed to be moving forward, an unrelated-yet-ominous, coincidental announcement was made; plans for a completely different type of mall – the Millcreek Mall, a $24 million, 125-unit fully-enclosed shopping center located on upper Peach Street in Millcreek Township and developed by the Cafaro Company – were announced on June 27.[37]

The June 29 groundbreaking on the new Hilton Hotel at the northwest corner of 10th and State streets served as another step for-ward for Tullio, and when the Concerned Businessmen's appeal of their previous lawsuit was rejected in August,[38] Mayer Brothers Construction Company broke ground on the Transitway Mall on Monday, August 13, 1973 at 11 a.m.; downtown State Street was closed to vehicular traffic immediately following the ceremony.[39]

▰ ▰ ▰

While the centerpiece of Tullio's desire to remake Erie may have been the Transitway Mall, in reality, commercial, industrial, and resi-dential redevelopment was occurring all across the city throughout his second term.

[34] "Seminar Explains Transitway Plan." Erie Morning News. 21 Nov. 1969: 13.
[35] Matthews, Ed. "Odds & Ends." Erie Times News. 5 Apr. 1970: C-2.
[36] "Hearing Scheduled on Transitway." Erie Times News. 4 Apr. 1973: VI 109.
[37] "Plans Unveiled for Millcreek Mall." Erie Times News. 26 Jun. 1973: VII 41.
[38] "Quick Mall Start Seen." Erie Times News. 4 Aug. 1973.
[39] "State Street to Close Monday." Erie Times News. 8 Aug. 1973: VII 87.

One obvious candidate for both aesthetic and practical renewal was the railroad line that ran down 19th Street.

In 1882,[40] the New York, Chicago, and St. Louis Railroad (nicknamed "The Nickel Plate Road") first laid tracks in Erie as part of an effort to connect Buffalo with Chicago. At that time the tracks – which ran right down the middle of 19th Street through densely-populated residential neighborhoods from Buffalo Road to Cranberry Street – were near the outskirts of town, but as the city grew around them, they became a dangerous inconvenience for generations of Erieites.

"The 19th Street tracks really divided this city, north and south, for 100 years," Horan said. "The reason we had to build all these fire houses on the other side, in south Erie, was because of the at-grade crossings."

There were 15 different places where Erie's streets crossed the 19th Street tracks – crossings that, at best, delayed residential traffic and emergency vehicles 10 to 12 times a day, and, at worst, presented frequent opportunities for pedestrian and vehicular accidents.

The Nickel Plate Road was absorbed by the Norfolk and Western Railroad in 1964, and not long after first taking office in 1965, Tullio began searching for ways to have five miles of the tracks – from Pittsburgh Avenue to East Avenue – removed or rerouted.

In 1970, Tullio received more Model Cities funding from President Nixon to explore the feasibility of removing the tracks.[41] In 1971, he returned to Washington to discuss the results of that study with former Massachusetts Governor and then-U.S. Secretary of Transportation John Volpe, who pledged his assistance with the matter.[42]

Tullio then met with representatives of the Norfolk and Western and the Penn Central Railroad in 1972 to discuss rerouting the 19th Street tracks, and possibly moving them right next to Penn's tracks between 14th and 15th streets,[43] and then met again with President Nixon in the fall of 1972 to update him on the progress.

Unfortunately for Tullio, the pace of that progress was slow; negotiating at the highest levels of government and business was laborious, and, for the time being, the 19th Street tracks – which, in 1972, were 90

---

[40] Guerriero, John. "19th Street Tracks Laid to Rest." Erie Times News. 15 May 2002. Retrieved 1 April 2015.
[41] "Tullio Seeks Funds For Track Removal." Erie Morning News. 5 May 1970.
[42] Ibid.
[43] Ibid.

years old – weren't going anywhere, except where they'd always gone: to Buffalo, and to Chicago.

Another commercial transportation-related initiative Tullio launched around the same time as the Transitway Mall and the 19th Street tracks removal was the creation of the Erie-Western Pennsylvania Port Authority.

The City of Erie Port Commission was created during the tenure of Mayor Art Gardner in 1956 with the mission to ensure that Erie would be ready to benefit from the expansion of the St. Lawrence Seaway. The Seaway – to be completed in 1959 – was a project that would widen an existing milieu of canals, locks, channels, and rivers stretching from the St. Lawrence River in Montreal to Lake Ontario. The Welland Canal, outside Buffalo, was also part of the project and would provide ample access from Lake Ontario to Lake Erie, giving larger cargo ships access to the Great Lakes from the Atlantic Ocean, and vice versa.[44]

The Port Commission began purchasing land along the Bayfront for the construction of a terminal that could accommodate the massive cargo ships that would soon come calling, as well as for the construction of launch ramps and related accommodations for recreational boaters.[45]

But in March 1973, Tullio was informed by Pennsylvania Secretary of Transportation Jacob Kassab that unless the city's Port Commission was converted to an authority, it would lose its annual $250,000 in state funding.[46]

Much like the historical dispute over half-century-old off-and-on plans to sell the city's water works, there was some contention over the creation of another so-called "lease-back" authority. Councilmen – and Tullio, for that matter – had to weigh the relative pros and cons of an "independent" authority that would no longer formally operate under the auspices of city government, but would consist of a board of 11 members, nine of which were to be appointed by the mayor.[47]

By June, an agreement in principle was reached, but some wrinkles still needed to be ironed out; councilmen were understandably wary[48] of Tullio's desire to exert such control over *any* proposed authority;

[44] Erie Western Pennsylvania Port Authority. n.d. 2 Apr. 2015. <http://www.porterie. org/about/>.
[45] Ibid.
[46] "Tullio Asks Council OK Port Authority." Erie Times News. 23 Mar. 1973.
[47] "Mayor Proposes Port Compromise." Erie Morning News. 29 Mar. 1973.
[48] Ibid.

despite Tullio's and council's general agreement that the authority was necessary, Tullio was willing to wait until he was sure that the $19 million, 17-year plans[49] for the port were in good hands – hands he'd appointed himself. Although state funding was no longer in jeopardy, a fully-operational authority for Erie's port wouldn't become a reality until 1974.

* * *

Following his wife Ceil's death just prior to his second term in 1969, Tullio threw himself into his work remaking Erie into a world-class city – but it wouldn't be long until wedding bells would again ring for the recently-widowed Tullio.

In January 1970, he went on a ten-day Caribbean cruise with his daughter Marilyn, where he met Grace Eileen Gunster[50] on the gang-plank during boarding. Gunster – a successful businesswoman who ran her family's business, the Herman Gunster Real Estate Agency[51] in Ridgewood, New Jersey – married Tullio on July 24, 1971[52] and joined him in Erie.

Unlike Tullio's first wife Ceil – who was supportive of but not en-thusiastic about Tullio's political career – Grace thrived on the excite-ment and enjoyed being Erie's new First Lady, to the point that she ordered a custom Pennsylvania license place that read GGT NO1.[53]

They did, however, have their differences. When they first met, Tul-lio invited her to accompany him as he presented the key to the City of Erie to the ship's captain; afterwards, he asked her to join him for a drink.

"I don't drink," she said.

Undaunted, he asked her to dance.

Grace responded that she "never felt at home" on a dance floor.

He offered her a cigarette.

"I don't smoke," she said.

---

[49] Thompson, Jim. "$19 Million Port Authority Plans Viewed." Erie Times News. 6 May 1973.

[50] Pintea, June. Author interview with June Pintea. 22 Jan. 2015.

[51] NorthJersey.com. Obituary: Grace Gunster Tullio, 95. 14 Feb. 2014. Retrieved 28 Jan. 2015.

[52] "Postnuptual Party Honors Mayor, Mrs. Tullio." Erie Times News. 11 Aug 1971.

[53] Tullio, John and Norma. Author interview with John and Norma Tullio. 15 Jan. 2015.

"I have two more questions to ask you," he responded. "What is your denomination, and what party are you registered with?"[54]

Grace was a Republican, and a devout Protestant.[55] "She was very strong in her religion," said Norma Tullio, Lou's sister-in-law and wife of Lou's brother, John. "She was always quoting from the Bible."[56]

Rather than focus on their divisions, Lou and Grace accepted their dissimilarities; when Grace would accompany her husband to the horse track, he would read the odds, and she, the Bible.[57] But Grace became something of a protector of Lou's,[58] for as he grew more powerful politically, there were bound to be people who would come for his job.

* * *

Mario Bagnoni was born[59] to Oreste and Doris Bagnoni on April 1, 1922 in Sarzana, Italy, which is about halfway between Genoa and Florence on the western, Mediterranean coast of Italy. He arrived in Erie with his family sometime prior to 1930 and served in the U.S. Coast Guard during World War II. Upon his return to Erie, Bagnoni performed as a big-band jazz guitarist[60] until life on the road began to wear on his wife.[61] He then joined the Erie Police Department, where he worked for 22 years, retiring as the Deputy Chief of Detectives in 1971.[62] After his retirement, Bagnoni – who lived in the Sixth Ward – would go on to serve as a city councilman for eight terms, the first of which commenced in 1972.

When Bagnoni – known to many as "Bags" – first arrived on council, he was seated alphabetically, right next to Councilman Cappabianca.[63]

"His legs would shake, that's how scared he was," said Cappabianca, who would reach over and grasp Bagnoni by the knee, holding his leg down to quell the tremors. "I would have to say, 'Bags, you're

[54] "Grace Tullio: First Lady." Erie Morning News. 23 Nov. 1988.
[55] Ibid.
[56] Ibid.
[57] Liebel, Patricia. Author interview with Patricia Liebel. 7 Jan. 2015.
[58] Wellejus, Ed. Author interview with Ed Wellejus. 13 Jan. 2015.
[59] Obituary: Mario S. Bagnoni. 6 Aug. 2005. Retrieved 22 Jan. 2015.
[60] National Music Museum. 24 Apr. 2014. Retrieved 11 Mar. 2015.
[61] Pallatella, Ed. "Mario Bagnoni has only one opponent left. Himself." Erie Times News. 21 May 2003. Retrieved 11 Mar. 2015.
[62] Ibid.
[63] Cappabianca, Pat. Author interview with Pat Cappabianca. 5 Jan. 2015.

alright, relax!' and I would grab him like that.'"

Much like Tullio, Bagnoni wasn't the most eloquent member of city government, but also much like Tullio, Bagnoni knew that a large part of remaining popular with voters was promptly responding to the concerns of his constituents.

"His whole forte was answering people's calls," Cappabianca said of Bagnoni, who, like Tullio, also kept his phone number listed the entire time he was in office. "People would call him, he'd answer, they'd go to the house, have coffee with him, he'd get back [to them]. He never refused a phone call and he always answered. That's what made Bagnoni. His thing was that he was a people person, a people's advocate. That's what elected him. And he was a little guy with a hat, like Mike Cannavino – doesn't speak well. People relate to that."

Bagnoni served his last five years in the Erie Police Department while Tullio was mayor, and the two reportedly enjoyed a close[64] relationship at that time.[65]

At some point, however, there was a falling out between Bagnoni and Tullio; speculation as to the reason for the split ranged from overtime wages Bagnoni supposedly was promised by Tullio but never paid[66] to Bagnoni's unrequited desire for further promotion during his law enforcement career.[67]

Whatever the case, Bagnoni would go on to become Tullio's greatest foil.

Tullio's greatest strengths as a politician, however, were that he didn't hold grudges,[68] and he always actively sought opportunities to turn enemies[69] into friends.[70]

There were enemies, to be certain, but they were dear and beloved enemies; dear and beloved in an honorable, Homerian way that Tullio the football coach and player could respect and, perhaps, grudgingly admire despite their oft-adamant opposition to his initiatives. Those dear and beloved enemies were players, playing the same game he was playing, and playing hard – yet they were never truly enemies, only fellow

---

[64] Wellejus, Ed. "Tullio and Bagnoni." Erie Times News. 19 Mar. 1972.
[65] Tullio, John and Norma. Author interview with John and Norma Tullio. 15 Jan. 2015.
[66] McKean, Edwin. Author interview with Edwin McKean. 23 Jan. 2015.
[67] Liebel, Patricia. Author interview with Patricia Liebel. 7 Jan. 2015.
[68] McKean, Edwin. Author interview with Edwin McKean. 23 Jan. 2015.
[69] Liebel, Patricia. Author interview with Patricia Liebel. 7 Jan. 2015.
[70] Wellejus, Ed. Author interview with Ed Wellejus. 13 Jan. 2015

competitors, and potential friends.

This is how he would play the wily Bagnoni, who'd opposed Tullio frequently and had already publicly contemplated a run for mayor less than a year after joining council.[71]

Instead of running, Bagnoni accepted Tullio's offer to join City Councilman Joseph Walczak, Jr. – who, in 1972 was also considering a mayoral try of his own[72] – as co-head of Tullio's 1973 re-election campaign.[73]

Practically speaking, Tullio couldn't have picked a better team – Walczak lived on the East Side in the Fifth Ward and was Polish, and Bagnoni lived on the West Side in the Sixth Ward and was Italian; Tullio's continued mastery of the ethnic factor in Erie politics would serve him well against the men who would soon come for his job.

Tullio's opponent in the May 15, 1973 Democratic Municipal Primary was again a familiar face – City Councilman Pat Cappabianca. Cappabianca was praised in some circles for standing up to a mayor that City Councilman Bernard Harkins had called "a dictator" in 1972.[74]

Consequently, Cappabianca ran as an anti-establishment candidate, telling the *Erie Morning News* shortly before the election that:

> "*When we started this campaign, some thought we were completely wasting our time, but we have narrowed it down so we're now neck and neck, and I believe we're going to be victorious Tuesday. We have had beautiful grass roots support – none of the professional politicians, but all good Erieites who have given much of their time and effort to return government to the people. If I haven't accomplished anything else, at least from now on any young man or young woman won't be afraid to toss his hat into the ring. My campaign and the support it has received will give heart to those who would fight the political machine.*"[75]

In the same *Erie Morning News* article, Tullio countered Cappabianca by touting his efforts to renew, rebuild, and redevelop Erie, much

---

[71] Pinksi, Jeff. "Bagnoni Considering Mayoral Try." Erie Morning News 13 Sept. 1972.
[72] "Walczak Thinking of Mayoral Run." Erie Morning News 14 Sept. 1972.
[73] Pinski, Jeff. "Bags, Walczak Touted to Head Tullio Drive." Erie Times News. 12 Jan. 1973.
[74] "Tullio Returns Harkins' Blast." Erie Morning News. 11 Aug. 1972.
[75] "Democratic Candidates for Mayor Speak Out." Erie Morning News. 15 May 1973.

like his friend and long-serving contemporary, Chicago Mayor Richard J. Daley – who'd visited Erie and Tullio in 1971[76] and was known to Chicagoans during his tenure from 1955 to 1976 as "King Richard the Builder" – had done in a similarly constituted Midwestern Great Lakes metropolis entangled by nickel-plated iron rails and perched at the western periphery of the Rust Belt that surrounded Erie.

"We worked very hard and I think we've had a very successful campaign and very clean campaign," Tullio said. "We've stuck with the issues and not with personalities. I think the vital issues in this campaign in this – in the eighth year of our administration, we've been very productive. I think we'll be known as the 'achievement administration.' All you have to do is look around the city and see the result."

Looking back on the election more than 40 years later, Cappabianca was succinct.

"I got killed," he said. "I really got slaughtered."

Cappabianca conceded[77] the race by 9:45 p.m. on election night – less than an hour after results began to reach the Tullio camp. Tullio won every city ward, and collected 16,973 votes to Cappabianca's 8,566.

Councilmen running for mayor could not run for reelection to council simultaneously, so Cappabianca – like Brabender before him – left city council and returned to teaching, becoming assistant principal at Gridley Elementary School. Tullio and Cappabianca didn't speak after the election for two years, until one day, newspaper headlines announced that Cappabianca could possibly lose his job after a parent took umbrage with the way Cappabianca had disciplined a student.

Sitting in his office at Gridley, Cappabianca's phone rang.

"Pat?" said the voice on the other end of the line.

"Yes?" Cappabianca answered.

"This is Lou."

"Lou who?" Cappabianca asked.

"Lou, you ass! The mayor!"

"Yes?"

"I saw the paper this morning, and I want you to know something," Tullio said. "If they let you go, you have a job with me."[78]

---

[76] "Here Come Da Mayors." Erie Times News. 1971 15 June.

[77] Thompson, Jim. "Tullio Scores Landslide: Third 4-Year Term Possible for Mayor." Erie Morning New.s 16 May 1973: 1.

[78] Cappabianca, Pat. Author interview with Pat Cappabianca. 5 Jan. 2015.

Lou's parents, Ersilia Nardoni Tullio and Anthony Tullio, probably around 1920. (*Courtesy of John and Norma Tullio*)

Wedding photo of Mary Cecelia McHale and Lou Tullio, circa 1940.
(*Courtesy of John and Norma Tullio*)

Tullio with composer Irving Berlin in the South Pacific during WWII. Because Tullio mailed this photograph home, his hand obscures information that may have been able to be used by the enemy to identify his location if intercepted. (*Courtesy of John and Norma Tullio*)

Tullio during the 1950s. (*Courtesy of John and Norma Tullio*)

Foreground, left to right: Ceil, Lou, and Ersilia Tullio on Tuesday, November 2, 1965 – the night of Tullio's first mayoral election victory over Mayor Charles Williamson. (*Courtesy of John and Norma Tullio*)

Louis J. Tullio For Mayor campaign business card, probably 1965. The obverse of the card says, "Lou's For You!" and lists his campaign address as 830 State Street. (*The Louis J. Tullio Collection of the Sister Mary Lawrence Franklin Archival Center, Mercyhurst University, Erie, Pa.*)

Tullio illustrating downtown redevelopment plans, late 1960s or early 1970s. (*The Louis J. Tullio Collection of the Sister Mary Lawrence Franklin Archival Center, Mercyhurst University, Erie, Pa.*)

A Tullio Press conference sometime between 1973 and 1975. (*The Louis J. Tullio Collection of the Sister Mary Lawrence Franklin Archival Center, Mercyhurst University, Erie, Pa.*)

Tullio welcomes President Jimmy Carter to Perry Square in fall 1980, just days before his loss to Ronald Reagan. (*The Louis J. Tullio Collection of the Sister Mary Lawrence Franklin Archival Center, Mercyhurst University, Erie, Pa.*)

Tullio, January 1978. (*The Louis J. Tullio Collection of the Sister Mary Lawrence Franklin Archival Center, Mercyhurst University, Erie, Pa.*)

In the mayor's office, January 1978. (*The Louis J. Tullio Collection of the Sister Mary Lawrence Franklin Archival Center, Mercyhurst University, Erie, Pa.*)

Lou and Grace Gunster Tullio, January 1978. (*The Louis J. Tullio Collection of the Sister Mary Lawrence Franklin Archival Center, Mercyhurst University, Erie, Pa.*)

Left to Right: Pat Liebel, Grace Tullio, unknown, Al Benedict, and Lou Tullio, attending the Democratic National Convention at Madison Square Garden, New York City in August, 1980. (*The Louis J. Tullio Collection of the Sister Mary Lawrence Franklin Archival Center, Mercyhurst University, Erie, Pa.*)

Tullio, riding a circus elephant up State Street, probably around 1983. An unverified anecdote states that when he was told he looked foolish atop the elephant, he replied with a classic Tullio-ism: "Let's just remember who's on top." (*The Louis J. Tullio Collection of the Sister Mary Lawrence Franklin Archival Center, Mercyhurst University, Erie, Pa.*)

Tullio circa 1985. (*The Louis J. Tullio Collection of the Sister Mary Lawrence Franklin Archival Center, Mercyhurst University, Erie, Pa.*)

In the mayor's office near the end of Tullio's tenure, probably 1987 or 1988. (*The Louis J. Tullio Collection of the Sister Mary Lawrence Franklin Archival Center, Mercyhurst University, Erie, Pa.*)

Tullio in 1988, speaking with Pennsylvania Governor Robert P. Casey – who would eventually lose his fight with Amyloidosis in 2000, like Pittsburgh Mayor Richard Caliguiri did in 1988 and Tullio did in 1990. (*The Louis J. Tullio Collection of the Sister Mary Lawrence Franklin Archival Center, Mercyhurst University, Erie, Pa.*)

Tullio at a photo shoot for Erie & Chautauqua Magazine in August 1988. (*Mark Fainstein*)

6

Strange Days

After the Municipal Primary Election of May 15, 1973, Lou Tullio still had an opponent to face in November. But in every election in which Tullio had been a candidate thus far, the circumstances were nothing resembling a "standard" one-on-one, Democrat-versus-Republican election.

He lost a tight primary election in 1965, only to waltz into office after the death of a competitor who'd beaten him in that primary election.

He decisively defeated token opposition in the 1969 primary.

He trounced a Democrat-turned-Republican in the general election six months later.

He "slaughtered"[1] a powerful fellow-Italian Catholic Democrat in the 1973 primary.

Now, in the fall of 1973, continuing the trend of "non-standard" elections, he would face an unconventional Republican opponent in what was certainly his strangest election ever.

---

[1] Cappabianca, Pat. Author interview with Pat Cappabianca. 5 Jan. 2015.

Richard Foht was born and raised in Erie; he graduated from Tech High School, dropped out of the Columbus College of Art and Design, returned to Erie, and then dropped out of Gannon. With the assistance of his brother Jack, he bought his first house and got into the real estate business as a landlord and speculator, but what he really wanted to do was to be involved in the national decision-making process, which led the then-27 year-old to challenge[2] the powerful two-term incumbent Tullio – who by then had been mentioned as a potential candidate for Governor[3] – in the November 1973 Municipal General Election.

"Frankly, there wasn't some burning desire to be mayor of Erie, but, [instead] to get involved in politics," Foht said[4] of his plans. "I saw that as an opportunity to possibly move on from there, to maybe congressmen or something along those lines."

It would be a stretch to consider Foht a serious challenger to Tullio. He raised no money, painted his own signs, and made his own bumper stickers. "You talk about grassroots, it doesn't get any grassier than that," he said.

To top it all off, Foht wasn't even a Republican.

"There's not a Republican bone in my body," said Foht. "I would've run as a Democrat from the get-go, but I knew that was totally crazy, because of the patronage, the entrenchment and so on and so forth."

Knowing he didn't have much chance of beating Tullio as a Democrat, Foht approached Republican County Party Chairman Gene Karnes and informed him that he'd be running for mayor as a Republican. Given the state of the local Republican Party at the time, Karnes and company were, as Foht said, delighted just to have a live body – a sacrificial lamb – to put on the ticket.[5]

Tullio treated Foht with kid gloves initially;[6] rather than unload on Foht with the full force of his fundraising, his friends, and his fearsome political acumen – which may have backfired by making Tullio look like a bully – Tullio went around calling Foht "a nice young man."[7]

Astutely, Tullio also rebuffed repeated requests from Foht to debate him.

[2] Foht, Richard. Author Interview with Richard Foht. 18 Apr. 2015.
[3] Wellejus, Ed. "Tullio for Governor?" Erie Times News. 30 Sept. 1973.
[4] Foht, Richard. Author Interview with Richard Foht. 18 Apr. 2015.
[5] Ibid.
[6] McKean, Edwin. Author interview with Edwin McKean. 23 Jan. 2015.
[7] Ibid.

"I think it was a smart thing to do – I mean, why give me more publicity?" Foht said.

Foht, however, was persistent, and even daringly interrupted a Tullio press conference to challenge him to a debate,[8] an offer that Tullio again refused.

"But I found an interesting way around that," said Foht. His solution was to place paid advertisements in the newspaper in the same font and same size type as real news articles. These advertisements were then structured to look like news coverage of debates between Foht and Tullio – debates that, in reality, never actually occurred. The only clue was at the bottom of the ad, where "PD ADV" – standing for "paid advertisement" – would appear.[9]

Tullio's answers to Foht's questions were written by Foht, and were actually non-answers. Each time Foht would present an issue, Tullio was portrayed as being unavailable to rebut, usually for some outlandish reason. "Lou – for one reason or another – had gone up to the bathroom, or was taking a drink from his water," Foht said. "I suppose from the standpoint then, it was just a smart-Alec thing that I was doing."[10]

Furthermore, Foht was outspoken in his criticism of the still-contentious Transitway Mall proposal,[11] and remained on the offensive against Tullio; in short, he wasn't acting like such a "nice young man" anymore, and Tullio responded by dropping the kid gloves.

Tullio began referring to Foht as a puppet of Karnes', joking that he didn't even know who his opponent really was – Karnes or Foht.[12]

Foht also began to believe that he was being followed by Erie police officers in unmarked cars.

"I had a habit of every day visiting the peninsula – that's really when I first noticed them," he said. "I don't think I would've noticed them otherwise. But every day, I take a ride out on the peninsula, and I started noticing that these unmarked-looking police cars were following me around the peninsula, so I knew that that was happening. They were keeping an eye on me."[13]

---

[8] Foht, Richard. Author Interview with Richard Foht. 18 Apr. 2015.
[9] Ibid.
[10] Ibid.
[11] "Exceptions Filed to Mall Ruling." Erie Morning News. 10 July 1973.
[12] "Tullio Calls Foht 'Karnes' Puppet." Erie Morning News. 14 Sept. 1973.
[13] Foht, Richard. Author Interview with Richard Foht. 18 Apr. 2015.

In September 1973, just a few weeks before the election, Foht attended a meeting at Gene Karnes' home to discuss financing his campaign. "It was probably around 3 o'clock in the morning I believe, and I left there. He lived on the lower East side, and at the meeting, I believe Tom Ridge was at that meeting – there were other principals in the Republican Party there – and to make a long story short... at the meeting, they told me, 'Sorry, sonny, there's no money there for you.' And they had really promised me that from the outset that there would be money."[14]

Upset, Foht began the short drive home to his residence near West Ninth and Cranberry streets. Encountering a flashing red light at South Park Row and State Street, Foht failed to come to a complete stop – just as an Erie Police Department cruiser was pulling out of the police garage a block away.

"And I mean, I was just going slow; I didn't want to get in an accident or anything, but, you know, 3 o'clock in the morning, nobody there – just keep on going," Foht said.

Correctly suspecting that the police officer had seen him roll the stop, Foht – who had been drinking alcohol at the meeting with Ridge and Karnes – decided to try to sneak home before the officer could pull him over.

"At the intersection of Ninth and Chestnut I went the wrong way on Chestnut, which would be to the north. I was going to try to pull the car in somewhere and make myself disappear," said Foht. The first car he encountered on Chestnut Street, travelling the *correct* way – southbound – was a police car. Foht had tried to outrun the police, and failed.

"You cannot drive faster than a radio," he said.[15]

The policeman who initially spotted Foht was the third or fourth officer on the scene, and was rather upset; he yanked Foht out of his Chevy Suburban while spewing obscenities at him.[16]

Then, while roughly placing Foht into the back of his cruiser, the officer "accidentally on purpose"[17] allowed Foht's face to come into

---

[14] Ibid.
[15] Ibid.
[16] Ibid.
[17] Ibid.

contact with the roof of the car; although Foht didn't think the police had specifically targeted him on this particular occasion, displayed on his bumper was a "Foht for Mayor" sticker.

He was taken to the police station in short order, charged with driving under the influence as well as several traffic violations, spent the rest of the night in jail, and walked home the next day.

"What happened in the aftermath of all that was, I offered my resignation to the Republican Party, and they declined to take that, and I finished off the race," he said. But from that moment on, according to Foht, the race was practically over.

▰ ▰ ▰

Earlier that year, however, an ugly incident occurred that would test Tullio, his family, his friends, his staff, and his employees. A lawsuit alleging impropriety on the part of Tullio's fundraising organization, called "The Mayor's Club," was filed, and not long after that action was initiated, the Internal Revenue Service came calling.

"That was really the brainchild – that whole thing was the brainchild of Gene Karnes,"[18] Foht said; although theories on who tipped off the IRS would range from his dear and beloved enemies Cappabianca or Bagnoni[19] to future Pennsylvania Governor Richard Thornburgh[20] – who was U.S. Attorney for the Western District of Pennsylvania at the time – Tullio would go to his grave never knowing who was behind the plot.

"They were really his ideas," said Foht of Karnes. "The lawsuit was filed by [future Pennsylvania Governor] Tom Ridge on Gene Karnes' behalf, and the audit was, you know, you'd only have to say something about an audit out loud and the IRS – it happens to perk up their ears, and they go and do it."

"I personally don't attribute motives to agencies," said Edwin McKean,[21] who served as Tullio's attorney throughout the audit. "I think that investigations can be initiated as a result of ill will, bad motives – not typically on the part of the agency – but a lot of investigations are initiated by third parties contacting the revenue service and making

---

18 Ibid.
19 Liebel, Patricia. Author interview with Patricia Liebel. 7 Jan. 2015.
20 McKean, Edwin. Author interview with Edwin McKean. 23 Jan. 2015.
21 Ibid.

allegations about a person, which then are considered by the agency, whatever agency it is, and if there appears to be a little smoke to it, why, that's when they commence an investigation."

And commence they did.

The Internal Revenue Service had, at the time, three divisions – a collections division, which was responsible for collecting delinquent taxes; an audit division, which received income tax returns, determined tax liability, and would occasionally audit returns; and a criminal investigation division, which was responsible for investigating and prosecuting tax crimes like failure to file tax returns, tax evasion, and other violations of the tax code. Agents from the criminal division work in tandem with an auditor,[22] and, according to McKean, a criminal investigator with a reputation for pursuing public figures was sent to live in Erie with the sole duty of scrutinizing Tullio.

"He [Tullio] was very disturbed, as anyone might be," McKean said. "His reaction to it was typical, the same reaction I would have or you would have. He wasn't irrational about it or hysterical or anything of that nature, he was just really disturbed that he was being investigated. He viewed it as an attack on his integrity, and he didn't take that lightly. He was at a loss as to why this was taking place. He – of course – denied any responsibility for anything that was a violation of the law, and that's how it began."

The source of contention in the investigation was a substantial deposit Liebel made to Tullio's personal account sometime in 1969.

"They engage in what's called a net worth analysis," said McKean of the IRS. "They determine what your net worth was at a certain date, and then they determine what your net worth is on a later date, and they subtract one from the other. And then they try to match up all your sources of money against that, and if your salary, wages, other dividends – all that sort of thing – are less than that amount, that increase in your net worth over that period of time, then they say, 'Where did you get this money?' And of course in this case there was more money than there was wages and that sort of thing. And there were a lot of different items that he had, and he couldn't remember what they were – and largely, he didn't know because Pat [Liebel] always took care of his affairs, and she couldn't remember. She was a busy girl, doing a lot of things, and running his office."

---

[22] Ibid.

The consequences of a conviction for Tullio would not only have ended his political career, but also could have landed him in the penitentiary.

"Being a public figure having been convicted of tax evasion – especially having been involved – he would've undoubtedly been sentenced to prison," McKean said. "And at that time in the Western District of Pennsylvania, there was a policy in the U.S. Attorney's Office and the District Courts to require a mandatory jail sentence for tax crimes. Those sentences would typically be a year and a day, and the defendant would serve some part of that, it might be as little as 30 days, it might be as much as a year. I've had clients receive both of those kinds of sentences. What would've happened in Lou's case? I can't tell you, but a public figure like that, he'd probably have been in jail."

According to both McKean[23] and Liebel,[24] the investigation was relentless. Virtually everyone who knew Tullio was contacted by the investigators, McKean said.[25]

"These revenue guys were frightening the hell out of ordinary local guys – in particular, there was a fella who worked at the [city] garage and just did odd jobs around the city, who had a gun pulled on him. Not pointed on him, but, you know, [the agent pulled his jacket aside and] uncovered the gun and that sort of stuff, and it scared the living daylights out of him."

"I thought people around him were being bullied unnecessarily – people who could've had no knowledge of, or connection to, [alleged] illegal activity. What they were attempting to determine," said McKean, "was whether anyone who was doing any contractual work for the city was actually – A, whether they paid Lou, and B, if these contracts were being fulfilled properly or the city was paying for but not getting the work that was supposed to be done."

As a result of the ongoing investigation, Tullio was dogged by rumors of corruption throughout the election year of 1973; it didn't seem to affect him during his primary contest with Cappabianca, and whether it was the fact that his general election opponent Foht was relatively weak and embroiled in a scandal of his own or the fact that the public still apparently had a great degree of faith in Tullio, the rumors didn't seem to affect him during the general election, either.

---

[23] Ibid.
[24] Liebel, Patricia. Author interview with Patricia Liebel. 7 Jan. 2015.
[25] McKean, Edwin. Author interview with Edwin McKean. 23 Jan. 2015.

Tullio defeated Foht by his largest margin of victory yet – out of almost 33,000 votes cast, Tullio claimed more than 22,000 of them. He won every city ward by more than double Foht's total except the Republican Fourth Ward, which Tullio won 2,272 to 1,358. Similar to Cappabianca's plight earlier in 1973, Foht could have won every city ward but the Fifth Ward by 20 percent and he *still* would have lost to Tullio, who again dominated his home ward – this time, by a margin of 8,050 to 3,266.

✂ ✂ ✂

As Tullio began his third term in January 1974 still ensnarled in his own David-and-Goliath battle against the IRS, he warned of forthcoming financial distress for the city;[26] Erie's municipal budget continued to expand, and a shrinking tax base was making it harder and harder to maintain balance.

He attacked both sides of the problem by attempting to reduce spending while simultaneously attempting to increase revenue with his Transitway Mall proposal, the expansion of Erie's port, and – early in 1974 – the proposal of a state-subsidized civic center. Unfortunately for Tullio, the returns on these initiatives were neither guaranteed nor immediate.

The Transitway Mall opened amidst much fanfare on September 23, 1974 – complete with inaugural ceremonies that included comedian Bill Cosby and '60s vocal pop quartet The Arbors[27] – although the impact of the whole endeavor would not be felt for some time. Ditto for the newly-established Erie Western-Pennsylvania Port Authority, which was finally realized that year, but would provide little in the way of immediate aid. Likewise, the proposed civic center was still but a pipe dream in the mid-70s.

Several of Tullio's other major projects remained in a state of limbo, including the removal of the 19th Street tracks, despite Tullio being invited to the White House to discuss the project with President Gerald Ford in 1975.[28] Additionally, the city's water works was then operating

---

[26] Thompson, Jim. "Tullio Inaugurated to Third Term; Vows 'Performance Administration.'" Erie Times News. 7 Jan. 1974.

[27] "Bill Cosby, Arbors to Appear at Downtown Mall Fete." Erie Times News. 8 Sept. 1974.

[28] "Tullio, Ford Meet Today." Erie Times News. 10 July 1975.

at a $500,000 deficit, and the city's overall budget was $522,000 short in June of 1975.[29]

With no instant salve for the city's financial woes in sight and the free-wheeling federal aid of the late-60s and early-70s beginning to dry up, Tullio faced the toughest challenges of his tenure; adding insult to injury, Tullio continued to deal with slightly less tangible problems.

◢ ◢ ◢

The Tonight Show Starring Johnny Carson was a television talk show hosted by Iowa-born comedian Johnny Carson from 1962 until 1992; Carson's homespun style, razor-sharp jocularity, and as-yet-unparalleled skill as an interviewer proved immensely popular from coast-to-coast – so much so that *Tonight* was named the 12th most popular television show of all time in 2002.[30]

It was on this momentous national stage that Erie resident – and City School Director Mary Lamary – would deal both her city and her mayor a most humiliating blow. Lamary happened to be in Burbank, California attending the National School Directors Convention, and was in the audience of Carson's show on April 11, 1973; during a question-and-answer segment with host Carson and comedian Jerry Lewis, Lamary asked them if they knew where the "mistake on the lake" was located. Both were baffled, so she mentioned that it was the city in which comedian Bob Hope had been married.[31]

"That must have been the mistake," Carson joked.[32]

Tullio was understandably upset and deemed Lamary's quip an insult.[33]

"It certainly doesn't speak well for an elected official," he said of Lamary's derogatory comment about Erie. "I've worked hard to tell regional and national audiences about the progress in Erie – new sewers to help clean up Lake Erie, and the attractive tourist industry... one swipe like that wipes out all of the progress we have made to improve Erie's image."[34]

---

[29] Thompson, Jim, and Dick Garcia. "Tullio, Hilinski Enter '75 With Matching Headaches." Erie Times News. 1 Jan. 1975.

[30] www.cbsnews.com. 2002. 16 Apr. 2015. <http://www.cbsnews.com/news/tv-guide-names-top-50-shows/>

[31] Thompson, Jim. "Lamary Quip Angers Erieites." Erie Times News. 14 Apr. 1973.

[32] Ibid.

[33] Horan, John. Author Interview with John Horan. 14 April 2015.

[34] Ibid.

Such was the self-inflicted stigma that many Erieites labored under; however, Tullio was correct in that progress *was* being made. Only eight days earlier, Erie had been named one of just 11 "All-America"[35] cities by the National Civic League – an organization founded by Louis Brandeis, Frederick Law Olmsted, and Theodore Roosevelt, among others, that had begun bestowing the award on cities in 1949 to recognize municipalities presenting innovative solutions to long-standing civic issues.[36] According to the National Civic League, the benefits of receiving an award include "national attention, a boost for recruitment of industry, jobs, and investments."[37]

"Why didn't she use the opportunity to tell them Erie is an All-American City and that Bob Hope was married in an All-American city?" Tullio lamented.[38]

Bolstering Tullio's claims of progress was the fact that in 1971, Tullio had been nominated – by his old friend, Chicago Mayor Richard J. Daley – to serve on the advisory board of the U.S. Conference of Mayors,[39] giving Tullio national recognition in a vast and powerful network of elected officials. The U.S. Conference of Mayors was, and is, a non-partisan organization comprised of mayors of cities across the United States with a population of 30,000 or more, charged with the promoting the development of effective urban and suburban policy, strengthening relationships between cities and the federal government, ensuring federal policy is in accord with urban needs, providing members with both leadership and management tools, and creating a forum for mayors to share ideas and information.[40] In 1973, Tullio was chosen as the organization's director.

By 1976, the cumulative effect of Tullio's nationwide connections as well as his desire to elevate Erie to a community of "national importance" like the one he referred to during his very first mayoral inauguration in 1966 had come to an easily foreseeable consequence – much

---

[35] "Erie Wins All-America Award As Top U.S. City." Erie Daily Times. 3 Apr. 1973: 1.
[36] The National Civic League. www.nationalcivicleague.org/2014. 29 Apr. 2015.
   <http://www.nationalcivicleague.org/>.
[37] Ibid.
[38] Thompson, Jim. "Lamary Quip Angers Erieites." Erie Times News. 14 Apr. 1973.
[39] "Tullio Nominated to US Mayors Post." Erie Times News. 14 June 1971.
[40] The Unites States Conference of Mayors. About USCM. 2015.
   <http://www.usmayors.org/meetmayors/mayorsatglance.asp>.

like his most recent mayoral opponent Richard Foht, Tullio felt that he could be of better service to Erie in Washington, D.C.; however, he'd have to get past a powerful, if oft-ridiculed congressman first.

🢒 🢒 🢒

Although Joseph Phillip Vigorito was born in Niles, Ohio in 1918, he found himself 100 miles to the north in 1938, graduating from Erie's Strong Vincent High School. He served in the United States Army during World War II, receiving a Purple Heart for his service; after the war, he earned a Bachelor's of Science from the University of Pennsylvania's prestigious Wharton School of Finance in 1947, and a Master's of Business Administration from the University of Denver in 1949.[41] Vigorito went on to teach economics at Penn State University Main Campus from 1949 to 1964,[42] when he was swept into office as part of the "Goldwater Class" of Democratic Congressmen who benefitted from President Lyndon Johnson's drubbing of Republican Barry Goldwater in that year's presidential election.

By 1976, Vigorito – an Italian who lived in Erie's Sixth Ward – had served six terms in the United States House of Representatives.

Despite his credentials, his education, and his experience, Vigorito was named as one of the "12 most outstanding non-entities in Congress" by *Washington Magazine* in 1972,[43] and also landed on *New Times* magazine's 1974 list of "10 dumbest congressman."[44] He was perceived by many as insignificant and ineffective, and after 12 years, had failed to pass even one bill of his own, mired as he was on the House Committee on Agriculture – a still-notorious dumping ground for the most uninfluential members of Congress. Following the disgrace of Nixon in 1974 and the short presidency of his successor, Republican Gerald Ford, the nation's political pendulum appeared to favor dramatic change prior to the 1976 presidential election; each of these factors made the heretofore-popular (in Erie, at least) congressman more vulnerable than ever.

---

[41] Biographical Dictionary of the United States Congress. Vigorito, Joseph Phillip. n.d. 19 Mar. 2015.
[42] Ray, Alex. Hired Gun: A Political Odyssey. Lanham, Maryland: University Press of America, 2008.
[43] "Tullio Announcement Seen." Erie Times News. 15 Jan. 1976.
[44] Brown, Warren. "Vigorito Gets Job Brushoff From Capitol." The Pittsburgh Press. 26 June 1977: A-28.

Tullio – with his larger-than-life political persona, as well as his now-expansive and mostly-successful experience in Washington – seemed to be a suitable opponent for Vigorito, despite Tullio's continuing involvement with the IRS and his difficulty in managing Erie's financial situation.

Murmurs of a Tullio congressional bid emerged as early as March 1975,[45] but by that summer, mixed signals appeared, hinting at a fourth mayoral term for Tullio instead.[46]

It wasn't until January 15, 1976 that he made his intentions clear.

Claiming that his fellow Democrat Vigorito was "not doing the job," while simultaneously lamenting a lack of leadership and alluding to Vigorito's status as a political non-entity, Tullio said in launching his campaign that Vigorito "has never been the author of an original piece of legislation which has become the law of this land."[47]

He went on to claim that of the average of 772 hours each year spent in debate by congress, Vigorito "has an average of five and a half minutes a year of debate out of those hours" and that he "did not debate any bill in Congress in 1972."[48]

"I can turn things around for the voters of this district," Tullio said.[49] Two others – Vincent DeLuca and Robert O'Hara – held similar sentiments and likewise joined the contest.

Although Vigorito was perceived as weak legislatively, he certainly wasn't weak electorally; as an entrenched, six-term incumbent, Vigorito had been a household name for regional Democratic voters for more than a decade – and, his reach was greater than Tullio's. At that time, Erie was part of Pennsylvania's 24th Congressional District, which included not only the City of Erie, but also Erie County, and parts of Mercer and Crawford counties, where many residents had no idea who this Lou Tullio even was.

Thus, it became clear to all that Tullio would have a tough time unseating Vigorito in the April 27 Congressional Primary Election unless he could carry the city by substantial margins as well as remain competitive in the outlying areas.

---

[45] Wellejus, Ed. "Tullio for Congress?" Erie Times News. 10 Mar. 1975.
[46] Wellejus, Ed. "Fourth Term for Tullio?" Erie Times News. 1 June 1975.
[47] "Tullio Announcement Seen." Erie Times News 15 Jan. 1976.
[48] Ibid.
[49] Ibid.

Tullio performed poorly almost everywhere[50] – including the city – and was trounced[51] by Vigorito.

He won just 14 of Erie's 71 electoral districts, and in doing so lost every ward in the city, including his home ward, the fifth. Adding to Tullio's miserable showing, the two other Democrats in the primary – DeLuca and O'Hara – did surprisingly well; in the city, Vigorito took 45.8 percent of the vote, Tullio took 38.2 percent, DeLuca took 9.7 percent, and O'Hara took 6.3 percent, meaning that in Erie, more people voted *against* Vigorito than for him.[52]

That was, however, not the case in areas outside the city; Vigorito received almost 20 percent more votes than his three opponents combined, and coasted to a decisive primary victory over his rivals – 51 percent to Tullio's 32 percent, with DeLuca and O'Hara claiming 10 percent and 6 percent of the vote, respectively. Vigorito's margin over Tullio was 12,000 votes.

A number of competing notions emerged as to why Tullio's not-so-shocking defeat became such a rout; however, careful analysis suggests that some of those theories can be dismissed out-of-hand.

While it is true that DeLuca and O'Hara siphoned a decent amount of anti-Vigorito votes away from Tullio, adding their totals – 6,417 and 3,980 respectively – to Tullio's 20,761 votes still wouldn't have helped him eclipse Vigorito's 32,761.[53]

Additionally, it could be reasonably supposed that Tullio's late start as a candidate – only about 100 days before the election – may have played a role in his staggering defeat; however, during his 5-day campaign against Mayor Williamson in 1965, Tullio demonstrated that his existing network of supporters was more than capable of rallying around him on short notice.

The strongest theory as to what really went wrong with Tullio's ill-starred congressional bid settles squarely – and strangely – upon that existing network of supporters.

[50] Garvey, William. "What Really Happened? A Political Analysis of the Tullio-Vigorito Democratic Primary." Erie Today Aug. 1976: 28-9, 41.
[51] "Vigorito Trounces Tullio." Erie Times News. 28 Apr. 1976.
[52] Garvey, William. "What Really Happened? A Political Analysis of the Tullio-Vigorito Democratic Primary." Erie Today Aug. 1976: 28-9, 41.
[53] "Vigorito Trounces Tullio." Erie Times News. 28 Apr. 1976.

Erie's Italians – as well as Erie's Polish, with whom Vigorito was popular[54] – faced an extremely simple choice: either replace one entrenched Italian (Vigorito) with another (Tullio), or vote against Tullio and retain *two* entrenched Italians; to that end, Tullio supporters may not have worked as hard as they could have to ensure that the previously well-oiled Tullio campaign machine continued to hum along at full speed. Tullio's ascension to congress would have meant a new mayor – with new friends and new enemies – and most certainly would have jeopardized the spoils of patronage many Tullio supporters had accrued by supporting him locally for over a decade.

Tullio himself may have sardonically bolstered this theory himself when asked about his "defeat."

"I just want to tell you I'm really glad, and all you people that wanted me to stay as mayor, I'm going to do your bidding," he said. "The people chose to keep me here as mayor and I respect that."[55]

---

[54] Garvey, William. "What Really Happened? A Political Analysis of the Tullio-Vigorito Democratic Primary." Erie Today Aug. 1976: 28-9, 41.

[55] Rush, Fred. Author interview with Fred Rush. 13 January 2015.

7

Simple Orchestrations

THE 1970S ENERGY CRISIS THAT HAD BEGUN IN 1973 PUSHED MUCH OF the western world into a two-year recession that signaled the end of the economic boom that followed World War II; the resulting unemployment, inflation, and general economic stagnation combined with the humbling withdrawal of American troops from the decades-long Vietnam War in 1975 made the mid-70s a particularly dour period in the history of the United States.

But in 1976, a much-needed morale-builder had luckily manifest itself in the collective consciousness of Americans. The 200-year anniversary of the start of the American Revolution spawned the United States Bicentennial Commemoration, and on July 4, 1976, parades, picnics, civic commemorations, and fireworks united communities across the nation in celebration.

Erie, however, wasn't one of those communities, and it wasn't until after the Independence Day holiday that many Erieites realized that the

City of Erie hadn't done much of anything.[1]

"There were fireworks [displays] all over, but the city didn't sponsor one," said City of Erie Housing Authority Executive Director John Horan.[2]

The executive director of Erie's volunteer-staffed bicentennial commission, G. Rodger Crowe,[3] insisted that his role was merely to coordinate the relatively-minor commemorations of local municipalities, not to create the events themselves; controversy arose when it was revealed that Crowe's salary of $10,000 – plus the salaries of an events coordinator and a secretary, which totaled $15,500 – could have easily paid for such a display. According to Horan, the media was "killing" Lou Tullio over the situation.[4]

"John, we have to do something," Tullio urgently said to Horan.[5]

What Horan and Tullio would come up with – initially known as "A Salute to the People of Erie" and held over Labor Day weekend in 1976 – would go on to become Erie's largest and most enduring yearly festival.

The way in which Tullio – who didn't really have much to do with Crowe's organization – handled the uproar over the circumstances again demonstrated his ability to turn difficult situations to his advantage.

Similarly, despite his loss to Vigorito in the congressional race as well as his continuing IRS troubles, things seemed to be mostly on track for Tullio as 1976 drew to a close; for the first time since 1973, a balanced preliminary budget (which came in at $17.6 million) was submitted for 1977. The Erie Hilton was completed in October, and the first steps towards creating the civic center complex – including the purchase of the former Sears building on French Street and the Warner Theatre on State Street – were being taken as well.[6]

Even Tullio's 11-year odyssey to remove the 19th Street railroad tracks seemed to finally be gathering steam. In March 1977, Tullio received word that the U.S. Rail Association had given permission for the

[1] "Quiet Bicentennial Sparks Controversy." Erie Morning News. 14 July 1976.
[2] Horan, John. Author Interview with John Horan. 14 April 2015.
[3] "Quiet Bicentennial Sparks Controversy." Erie Morning News. 14 July 1976.
[4] Horan, John. Author Interview with John Horan. 14 April 2015.
[5] Ibid.
[6] Grazier, Jack. "Good Year For Lots of Things, Including Controversy." Erie Times News. 28 December 1976: 12-B.

Norfolk and Southern tracks to be moved right next to Conrail's, which ran between 14th and 15th streets.[7]

"It seems fairly simplistic now," Horan said of Tullio's orchestration, "but trying to get a competitor to agree to allow you to run your railroad along their tracks – I mean it's incredible when you really think about it."[8]

Later that spring, Tullio would coast to his largest margin of victory in a primary election ever, again facing Richard Foht – this time, as a Democrat, in the primary election.

Foht – whose 1973 arrest resulted in an acquittal when defense attorney Tom Ridge located a witness who observed, from a second-floor apartment across the street, the police officer manhandling Foht – lost every ward *and* every district to Tullio, who won the election by more than 40 percentage points.

His political aspirations now dashed, Foht echoed Richard Nixon's quote upon losing the California gubernatorial election to incumbent Pat Brown in 1962 when he told[9] the *Erie Times-News*, "Well, you won't have Richard Foht to kick around anymore." All joking aside, Foht moved to South Carolina shortly thereafter, became a successful businessman, and never again dabbled in Erie politics.[10]

That summer, in a nod to the recently-created but already iconic "I Love New York" advertising campaign created by graphic designer Milton Glaser in 1977,[11] "A Salute to the People of Erie" was renamed "We Love Erie Days."[12]

Not long after the celebration, Tullio again trounced a less-than-formidable electoral opponent, ensuring himself an unprecedented fourth term as the Mayor of Erie. Robert Doutt – who heavily criticized Tullio's handling of the city's pension fund[13] – lost every ward to Tullio in spectacular fashion. In the first and second wards, Tullio tripled Doutt's totals. In the third and fourth, he doubled Doutt. In the Sixth Ward, Tullio carried the day by more than 4,000 votes, and in the Fifth Ward

---

[7] Grazier, Jack. "Track Removal Almost Certain, Tullio Believes." Erie Times News. 9 Mar. 1977.
[8] Horan, John. Author Interview with John Horan. 14 April 2015.
[9] "Foht Quits Politics." Erie Times News. 18 May 1977.
[10] Foht, Richard. Author Interview with Richard Foht. 18 Apr. 2015.
[11] Ibid.
[12] "Mayor Plans Erieland Celebration." Erie Times News. 7 July 1977.
[13] "Tullio Defends Pension Against Doutt's Claims." Erie Times News. 20 Oct. 1977: 22-a.

– still truly Tullio's turf – he prevailed by more than 5,000. In total, Tullio's 26,781 votes were the most he'd ever earned, and his margin of 15,438 votes was his greatest yet.

"I'm going into my fourth term and in that time," Tullio said, "you're bound to please some and displease others. But more must be pleased than displeased."[14]

▰ ▰ ▰

Tullio's good fortune would continue; shortly after winning his fourth term in 1977, he presented an $18.6 million budget for 1978; although it contained a small deficit,[15] it proved that Tullio's time in office had taught him how to wrestle the city's finances at least to an impasse.

As Erie emerged from the mid-70s economic malaise, the Tullio administration hit what was probably in retrospect its high-water mark. Things seemed to be progressing as well as they ever would, politically, and in early 1978, Tullio would finally get the redemption he'd been seeking personally.

"This investigation went on for five years," said Ed McKean of the politically-motivated IRS audit Richard Foht[16] claimed was instigated by Republican County Chairman Gene Karnes. "It was unrelenting during that period of time. Those two agents lived in Erie for five years and chased him. They tried to find something on him."[17]

They never did.

"Pat [Liebel] took an enormous amount of abuse during this investigation; she was called down to the grand jury in Pittsburgh and subjected to just unreasonable attacks on her personal honor as well as a refusal on the part of the US Attorneys to accept what she said," McKean said.[18] "She never had any knowledge of any violation of any kind of the law by the mayor and she certainly wasn't engaged in any of those [alleged] activities."

"It was just ridiculous," said Liebel.[19] "I was at the grand jury three times... the third time I was there, the judge [Gerald Weber] who was presiding looked at the US Attorney and he said, 'Unless you

---

[14] "Foht Quits Politics." Erie Times News. 18 May 1977.
[15] McKinney, Bill. "Tullio to Present '78 Budget to Council." Erie Morning News. 30 Nov. 1977.
[16] Foht, Richard. Author Interview with Richard Foht. 18 Apr. 2015.
[17] McKean, Edwin. Author interview with Edwin McKean. 23 Jan. 2015.
[18] Ibid.
[19] Liebel, Patricia. Author interview with Patricia Liebel. 7 Jan. 2015.

have something different to ask Miss Liebel, she is being excused from this grand jury.' And he said, 'Well I don't have anything new,' and he [Judge Weber] said, 'Then, I'll tell you this,' and he looked right at the US Attorney's face and said, 'I don't ever want to see that woman before this grand jury again.' And so I was happy as a lark when I walked out."

"She was very loyal to Lou," McKean said of Liebel. "Very devoted, but also very able. And it was Pat who uncovered the source of some money that I was unable to identify for a long, long period of time."

Back then – in what was an acceptable political practice that is rather questionable today – it was something of a tradition to slip a few dollars in a prayer card at a funeral, and leave it with the family.

"Well, Lou – being the mayor of the city – he had an awful lot of people call at the time of his first wife Ceil's death," McKean said. "And people left money in these envelopes and it amounted to a fair amount of money. And it was deposited to Lou's account. Now, he didn't make the deposit; Pat did. She took care of all of his personal stuff, you see. And no one could remember where this money came from including Pat. Everyone scratched their heads. Here we had a substantial deposit into Lou's bank account and at a period of time that he was being investigated, and we were unable to identify the source of it."[20]

McKean's recollection is that Liebel was "rooting around" at Tullio's home one day, going through records, found the envelopes, and made the connection.[21]

"On each envelope as I remember it was written the amount of the gift. When you added them all up they came to the exact amount of the deposit. [So] that problem was solved."

The fruitless IRS investigation ended abruptly, and on a puzzling note.

"He found out by a letter," said McKean. "I got aggravated at the time because I wasn't even copied on it. And that was a violation of – that letter should've come to me in the first place. But it didn't. He said 'I got this letter. What does this mean? Is it over?'"[22]

---

[20] McKean, Edwin. Author interview with Edwin McKean. 23 Jan. 2015.
[21] Ibid.
[22] Ibid.

The letter contained a simple one-sentence statement that said little more than that the investigation was being terminated.

"Most tax investigations, in fact every tax investigation I was ever involved in was conducted by a CID agent from the Erie office of the Internal Revenue Service. I knew those guys. They were all very competent men," McKean said. "They were very competent people. Honorable. Very difficult adversaries. But I had a good working relationship. I knew all of them. And, I would've received a phone call if an investigation was being terminated. I would be told by an agent. I don't ever recall receiving a letter on any investigation of the kind that Lou received."[23]

It could be supposed that the terse, brief notification to Tullio (but not McKean) might indicate frustration on the part of the agency in being unable to find prosecutable behavior by Tullio; whatever the case, one of the toughest chapters of Tullio's tenure was now over.

"I'm here to tell you that if there's anybody on the face of the Earth who knew [if Tullio had engaged in illegal activity], it was me," said McKean. "He *never* took a nickel from anybody. He was a straight shooter and I admire the man for that."[24]

Another puzzling – and somewhat humorous – aspect of the conclusion of the IRS investigation was that not only did the IRS fail to find evidence of wrongdoing on Tullio's behalf, what they *did* in fact uncover during the five-year assault on his integrity ended up making the IRS look like the wrongdoers. "When they got all done," McKean said, "my recollection is Lou got a tax refund."[25]

▰ ▰ ▰

Building on the successes of 1978 was Lou Tullio's goal in 1979; he referred to 1978 as a "productive year" and touted accomplishments including $2.5 million in sewer improvements, the construction of the Chestnut Street and East Avenue boat ramps for $150,000, and $2.89 million in grants to local businesses for development and expansion – none of which came from the city's coffers, but instead from the federal sources Tullio had been so astute in tapping.[26]

[23] Ibid.
[24] Ibid.
[25] Ibid.
[26] Tullio, Lou. "A Very Productive Year for Erie." Erie Times News. 28 Jan. 1979: 12 G.

Tullio also talked about future requests for funding, including $3 million for the renovation of the Sears building and the Warner Theatre as part of the proposed civic center complex, $1.5 million for capital improvements, $4 million for street repairs, and $1.4 million for a waste disposal system.[27]

Imperfections, however, began to appear in the tone of Tullio's tune; the city's $20 million budget for 1979 required a two-mill property tax increase,[28] the Transitway Mall was shaping up to be a tremendous disaster – as evidenced by the closing of downtown department store giant The Boston Store[29] – and the city's water department continued to post regular losses.

In August, a resolution was brought before City Council calling for the creation of an independent water authority;[30] oddly, the blame for the water department's poor performance fell squarely on Tullio, who had advocated for the creation of just such an authority for almost his entire political career and had been beaten back time and time again.

Stranger still, the resolution came from Tullio's greatest adversary – Mario Bagnoni.

"I want to take the water department out of the mayor's hands completely," said Bagnoni. "He's had it since he took office and he's done a hell of a lousy job with it."[31]

"I've backed the authority concept all my life," said Tullio, who went on to complain that he was disappointed that it had taken council so long to come around to his way of thinking on the matter, and that Bagnoni's plan wouldn't work.[32]

"He doesn't know what he's talking about," Bagnoni replied.[33]

Although nothing came of the resolution, the barbed jabs traded by Tullio and Bagnoni illustrated perfectly the scope and severity of the stresses between the two aging competitors at this stage of their respec-

---

[27] Ibid.
[28] "City Real Estate Tax Increased by Two Mills in 1979 Budget." Erie Times News. 27 Dec. 1978: 1.
[29] "Mayoral Priorities Picked." Erie Morning News. 12 June 1979.
[30] "Bagnoni, Tullio Clash Over Water." Erie Morning News. 21 Aug. 1979.
[31] Ibid.
[32] Ibid.
[33] Ibid.

tive careers.

Bagnoni was thought by some to be a professional "againster"[34] who made a career out of opposing Tullio.

"Bagnoni was for Bagnoni," said his contemporary, Pat Cappabianca. "Bagnoni didn't like to be crossed in any way. He had to have his own way, every time."[35]

Tullio, however, continued to handle Bagnoni adeptly, as Tullio's attorney Ed McKean remembers.

"I recall on one occasion being at his home for dinner, and Lou – who was a pretty good cook – and his second wife and I were having dinner and he had fixed pork chops, if I remember. And the phone rang, and Lou always answered the phone no matter who was calling. No one screened his calls. He'd just pick the phone up. He did the same thing at the office."[36]

On the phone was Bagnoni, who was yelling at Tullio loud enough that McKean and Grace – still seated at the dinner table – could hear him from across the room.

"Yes, Mario," Tullio was overheard to say. "I'll look into it. Yes, Mario. Yes, Mario. Good night, Mario. Nice to hear from you, Mario."

"Lou, how can you be nice to that man?" Grace asked.

That, said, McKean, was Lou Tullio in a nutshell.

"He'd see Mario the next day at City Hall, and say, 'Hi Mario! How are you?' And I think Mario was very perplexed by all that. But, that's Lou."[37]

Tullio's skill in handling Bagnoni would be put to the ultimate test when, in January 1981, Bagnoni announced his intentions to run for mayor.

"He has not been listening to the wants and needs of the people," said Bagnoni of Tullio. "He's been listening to the Manufacturers' Association and the Erie Conference, not to the average worker."[38]

Alluding to the David-and-Goliath strategy of the fight he was about to enter, Bagnoni said, "I won't have rocks in my slingshot, just the truth."[39]

[34] Wellejus, Ed. Author interview with Ed Wellejus. 13 Jan. 2015.
[35] Cappabianca, Pat. Author interview with Pat Cappabianca. 5 Jan. 2015.
[36] McKean, Edwin. Author interview with Edwin McKean. 23 Jan. 2015.
[37] Ibid.
[38] "Tullio Has 'Mixed Emotions.'" Erie Morning News. 15 Jan. 1981.
[39] Ibid.

Truth or not, Bags came out slinging.

He demonized Tullio for rewarding allies with political jobs in his administration, and savaged Erie Police Chief Richard Skonieczka – and Tullio by association – for mishandling the investigation into the suspicious unsolved murder of Erie Police Officer Corporal Robert Owen[40] as well as for mismanaging the police force in general.

"I'm not worried," said Tullio of Bagnoni's assertions.[41]

Tullio responded with assertions of his own, albeit of a much more positive nature; the power of incumbency – in the absence of gross misconduct of a moral or financial nature – means that incumbents can usually point to achievements rather than giving up ground by slinging mud.

The first phase of a $40 million downtown redevelopment project centered around the Erie Insurance campus had begun in 1980, as had a $2 million development project at Bucyrus Erie. An expanded effort to engage minority contractors produced positive results, the Housing Authority of the City of Erie under John Horan was making significant improvements to the quality of Erie's housing stock, Erie's sewer system had just received $4 million in improvements,[42] and ground was broken on the civic center complex.[43]

Despite these achievements, Tullio had proven in the past he wasn't always the type to kindly abide abuse. Shortly before the May 19, 1981 Democratic Municipal Primary, he addressed the Kiwanis Club.

"I'd like to read a letter sent by Bagnoni when he retired from the police department in 1970 to then- Chief of Police Charles Bowers," he told them.

Producing Bagnoni's letter, Tullio then read it aloud.

"I believe that Mayor Tullio has been one of the finest mayors under whom I have served, and he has done more for the Erie Police Department as a whole than any previous mayor," it said.[44]

Roaring with laughter, the Kiwanians gave Tullio a standing ovation.[45]

For as much as Tullio had going for him, the ethnic factor in Erie

[40] Pasquale, Tony. "Chief Defends Police, Raps Bagnoni for Criticism." Erie Morning News. 23 April 1981.
[41] "Tullio Has 'Mixed Emotions.'" Erie Morning News. 15 Jan. 1981.
[42] Tullio, Lou. "Projects Keep Erie Moving." Erie Times News. 25 Jan. 1981: 2-L.
[43] "Groundbreaking Galore!" Erie Morning News. 21 April 1981.
[44] "Bagnoni Letter Praises Mayor Tullio." Erie Times News. 6 May 1981.
[45] Ibid.

politics was still at play; Tullio and Bagnoni were both Italian Catholics, and would certainly split the supporters who constituted their respective bases; Tullio supporters expected to handily defeat Bagnoni by at least a two-to-one margin.[46]

In reality, the race would be much, much closer.

Bagnoni lost by only 1,269 votes, 13,891 to 12,622. It was Tullio's closest victory ever – even closer than his 3,833-vote triumph over Williamson in 1965; it was also his second-closest election ever, with his 1965 primary loss to Cannavino by 873 votes remaining the tightest race Tullio had ever experienced.

"It shows a lot of people aren't happy with the way the administration is running the city," Bagnoni said.[47]

Bagnoni's assertion may hold some validity, but it's also likely that voters simply had to choose between two candidates who were, much like in the Tullio-Vigorito proposition, more or less well-liked; in this case, a defeated Bagnoni could go back to council, but a defeated Tullio could only go back to his tree-shaded home on East Grandview Boulevard.

A deeper analysis of the results indicate just how difficult this choice was for some. Bagnoni became the first candidate to actually win an entire ward against Tullio in more than a decade – Bob Brabender took the Republican Fourth Ward in 1969 – when he beat Tullio by *one vote* in the Second Ward, 1,089 to 1,088. In his own home Sixth Ward, Bagnoni also prevailed, but by just 44 votes, 3,852 to 3,808.

In the First Ward, Tullio bested Bags by but 81 votes, 1,508 to 1,427. In the Third Ward, Tullio gained some breathing room with a 217-vote victory, 1,227 to 1,010. The Fourth Ward added to Tullio's lead, where he prevailed 1,318 to 973.

Tullio's old bastion of strength – the Fifth Ward – once again delivered the largest margin of the election (671 votes), granting Tullio 4,942 votes to Bagnoni's 4,271.

"I'm very happy to have won," said Tullio. "I think the people of this city were very intelligent and fair."[48]

"I didn't have any illusions," Bagnoni said. "I told you people it

---

[46] McKinney, Bill. "Tullio Wins Dem Primary After Hard-Fought Battle." Erie Morning News. 20 May 1981: 1.
[47] Miller, George. "Cannavino Becomes First Candidate for Mayor." Erie Times News. 29 Nov. 1988.
[48] Ibid.

was like David taking on Goliath."[49]

Goliath also had a lesser David to face that fall; continuing his trend of anti-climactic Municipal General Elections, Tullio took on a little-known Republican by the name of Ed Hammer and unsurprisingly nailed him. Tullio won every ward by at least double Hammer's totals – sometimes triple. Hammer – who spent all of $102 on his campaign – failed to earn more than 800 votes in four of the city's six wards, leading to an 18,716 to 6,160 defeat.

"It's a great vote of confidence," Tullio said, perhaps alluding to his narrow victory over Bagnoni in which more people had voted against him as an incumbent than ever before.

With that vote of confidence also came a protest vote – his margin over Doutt in 1977 was his greatest, at 15,438, but his margin over Hammer, at 12,556, ended his trend of ever-increasing general election vote totals. One explanation for this slight slip in support probably traces its roots back to Bagnoni – who received 3,266 write-in votes.[50]

After Tullio's high-water point of 1978, the election of 1981 marked a major change in his administration; although he survived his first real challenge to power in 16 years, discord in the composition of the existing ethnopolitical structure was audible – Tullio was still the maestro, but the band was now playing different tunes, his understudy waiting in the wings.

---

[49] Ibid.
[50] Sanfilippo, Vicki. "Lynch Already at Work; Johnson Gracious Loser; Tullio Beats Hammer 3 to 1." Erie Daily Times. 4 Nov. 1981:

8

A New Beginning

THE ETHNIC FACTOR IN ERIE POLITICS WAS BORN OF A PARADIGM THAT was still relevant in the first half of the 20th century – established Scotch-Irish-English and German Protestants competing against newly-arriving Italian, Polish, and Irish Catholics.[1] Lou Tullio had been the first to truly break through that orange ceiling, becoming the first Italian Catholic mayor of the City of Erie in 1966; the ruling ethnic coalition at that time, however, had neither considered nor included non-Christians, non-Europeans, or women as formidable constituency groups until their respective liberation movements in the 1970s.

It's hard to describe such notable firsts as the 1968 election of attorney Leonard Ostrow as the first Jewish City Councilman or the 1978 election of attorney Larry Meredith as the first African-American City Councilman as proof of the "socioeconomic maturation," of these constituencies, because these groups had been gaining strength for decades, and, as in the case with women, were actually *not* a minority; the political power of these groups had been limited by tradition, and, in some cases, by considerations both *de facto* and *de jure*; thus, the maturation indeed

---

[1] Garvey, William P. PhD. The Ethnic Factor in Erie Politics. University of Pittsburgh, 1973.

was not in these overlooked, underserved, fully-developed constituency groups, but instead in the electoral system's ability to accept them.

As Tullio began his historic fifth term in 1982, that paradigm – one that had existed since the earliest days of the United States – was changing. Long-time Tullio foe Bernard "Babe" Harkins – who'd been on council since 1964 but for one brief interregnum from 1976 to 1978 – was now gone, and was replaced by the first woman ever elected to the Erie City Council.

Joyce Savocchio was among the second generation of her family to be born in Erie;[2] her parents – themselves children of Italian immigrants who hailed from Rocca Pia, Abruzzi, 75 miles east of Rome – operated a grocery store on the outskirts of Little Italy where a young Joyce would learn her first political lessons.

"We lived over the store and the neighborhoods were very close knit," she said.[3] "And so, you got to know all of your neighbors; they probably could have written a book about the things that happened in our store. I think that played a large part in my development – I think you look back on things, and you see the influence."

That family store was also where she would first meet Tullio, thanks to her politically-active father.

"I grew up in that [political] environment," said Savocchio. "He and Lou Tullio had become good friends. I can recall Lou Tullio at a fairly young age, before he became mayor, and never knowing that one day I would be serving on a council with him as mayor."[4]

Savocchio attended Irving Middle School and Roosevelt Middle School before moving on to Strong Vincent High School, where her own political interests began to coalesce.

"During my high school years, [when] I was a junior, I was reading a Scholastic Magazine," she said. "Every kid that went to public schools – I don't know about the parochial schools – you got a Scholastic Magazine once a month in your history class. I had heard about [Massachusetts Senator John F.] Kennedy, but I never really knew much about him and I read this article."[5]

Impressed, Savocchio thought, "This is fantastic. I've got to find out

---

[2] Savocchio, Joyce. Author Interview with Joyce Savocchio. 20 Apr. 2015.
[3] Ibid.
[4] Ibid.
[5] Ibid.

more about this man."[6]

She began researching Kennedy, and when he announced his candidacy for president, she became a "Kennedy Girl," which was a nationwide club consisting of a youthful contingent of campaign supporters who volunteered their time going door-to-door, working at campaign offices, hosting rallies, and, in some cases, doing advance work for campaign visits.

"I learned a lot during that campaign," said Savocchio. "We were warned that – when we were going door to door – we could be abused in some way. And I can recall unbelievable language, doors being slammed in my face. One guy actually spit on me, and it was because he [Kennedy] was Catholic and [if Kennedy won it was feared that] the Pope was going to run the country! I think it was a great experience for somebody who was young that had had a pretty sheltered life in terms of prejudice, although I had experienced it in my own life. Not only in my life as a woman, but as an Italian-American."[7]

Prior to Tullio's first election in 1965, Italians, Catholics, and pretty much anyone with a vowel at the end of their last name could still sometimes be discriminated against by the old order; Tullio was a local pioneer in alleviating some of that discrimination, however, until Savocchio's election to council, traditional gender roles still dictated that in the city of Erie, politics was no place for a woman. Even in high school, Savocchio felt the effects[8] of that stereotype; she recalls a history teacher at Strong Vincent who was in charge of holding a simulated Kennedy-Nixon debate using students as the candidates.

"I desperately wanted to do it," she said. "I was absolutely captivated by Kennedy; I was very sure that he was going to win, and I guess this was my way of saying, 'I can help him win by doing this debate.'"[9]

Savocchio volunteered for the role of her idol Kennedy, and was heartbroken when another young man was chosen instead.

"I went up, and – I don't know where I got this courage at the time – and I said, 'I know why you did this. You did this because I'm a woman.' And I said, 'I want you to know that I could have done a better job.'

Two days later, the young man backed out of the debate, leaving

---

[6] Ibid.
[7] Ibid.
[8] Ibid.
[9] Ibid.

that history teacher a chance to atone for his mistake.[10]

"He came to me, and I said, 'You know, I should really say "no" because you made that decision based on my sex.' But I said, 'I'm not doing this for you, I'm doing this for John F. Kennedy.' And I did it and I won. And to me that was a very clear indicator that it was going to be a victory for John F. Kennedy."

It was indeed a victory for Kennedy over Nixon, in the closest presidential contest since Woodrow Wilson's in 1916; more importantly for Erie, it was a victory for Savocchio, who was now armed with the knowledge that stereotypes of the time couldn't constrain her.

"I remember being on stage, and something just connected. I don't know what made me say it to myself but I said, 'I'm going to run for office.' I don't know what made me say it at that point. I think I was so, just, struck with the idea of Kennedy. He inspired so much. He inspired my entire generation to public service of different kinds and I even mentally said to myself, 'I am going to be the first woman elected to City Council.'"[11]

Savocchio went on to earn her Bachelor's Degree in History with a minor in Education from Mercyhurst College (now University), where she also served as class president; from there, she went to Pitt for her Master's Degree in Education, where her thesis dealt with the subject of Tullio as a transitional mayor.[12]

Later, after working as a teacher in the Erie School District, she earned what would today be called a Master of Public Administration from Edinboro University, continued teaching, as served as president of the Erie Teachers (later, Erie Teaching) Association.

By the late 1970s, Savocchio had contemplated a run for Erie City Council.

"Over the years, I taught so many kids that would say to me, 'Ms. Savocchio, you should run for office.' I'm thinking, 'What are they thinking? They just want me out of here?'"

After she considered the move, she went to talk to Tullio – who she'd gotten to know even better while she was working on her thesis at Pitt.

"If you ever run, Joyce," Tullio told her, "you come and let me

[10] Ibid.
[11] Ibid.
[12] Ibid.

know."[13]

Savocchio promised to do so.

"I don't think this is the right time for you to run," he then told her when that time had come. Harkins' seat seemed to be safe, and Tullio wanted Larry Meredith to remain on council,[14] leaving little room for Savocchio.

"Well, I understand your feelings about that," Savocchio said. "But I think you misunderstand my reason for this visit. The visit isn't to negotiate whether I'm going to run or not. It's that I'm keeping my promise and letting you know that *I am* running."

According to Savocchio, Tullio was "a little bit taken aback" by her determination.

"I honestly think he didn't think I had a snowball's chance in hell," she said.[15]

Savocchio did run, and won, becoming – as she'd long-ago predict-ed – the first woman elected to Erie City Council.

Just prior to her inauguration on January 4, 1982, however, the outgoing council passed one of the ugliest municipal budgets to date. On New Year's Day, 14 hours past the December 31 deadline, Erie City Council took just four minutes[16] to approve a $26 million budget by a vote of five to two; Harkins and Bagnoni were the only ones to object to the 4.5 mill property tax increase, which pushed the total to 27.5 mills.[17]

The drastic growth in both property taxes and spending meant that Savocchio was entering this new era as municipal government was be-coming more and more handcuffed, financially.

January 4, 1982 was also the day of Tullio's inauguration to his fifth term as mayor; in his address at the ceremonies held that day, he – for the very first time – counted Bayfront redevelopment among his administration's top priorities for the coming year.[18] For Erie's fiscal handcuffs, however, he blamed "the stinging blade of inflation," as well

[13] Ibid.
[14] Liebel, Patricia. Author interview with Patricia Liebel. 7 Jan. 2015.
[15] Savocchio, Joyce. Author Interview with Joyce Savocchio. 20 Apr. 2015.
[16] "Council Passes City Budget in 4 Minutes." Erie Times News. 2 Jan. 1982.
[17] Ibid.
[18] "Tullio Enters Historic Fifth Term as Mayor." Erie Morning News. 5 Jan. 1982.

as the decline in President Ronald Reagan's federal funding to cities for the city's imperiled financial situation.[19]

What he didn't say, however, was that the city's budget had actually *remained stable* in comparison to 1966 once inflation was factored in to the equation. The approximately-$9 million budget Tullio inherited in 1966 would, in reality, cost right around $26 million in 1982 dollars; with his current budget right at $26 million, Tullio had effectively controlled city spending while not only continuing to provide services but also continuing to address some of the root problems on the revenue side of the budget equation.

"Everyone has the basic right to live in dignity. We will look for new avenues to explore and ways to serve our fellow man," he said, while again referencing his long-held desire (referenced in his very first inaugural address some 16 years prior) to make Erie "the greatest city in the Commonwealth and in the nation."

The only person of note absent from the inaugural ceremonies that day was Mario Bagnoni.[20]

🖋 🖋 🖋

Tullio would begin his fifth term – just short of his 66th birthday – on the operating table.[21]

He had had minor cataract surgery in 1972, however this was a much more serious procedure – open heart surgery. Testing the previous summer revealed an unknown number of coronary artery blockages,[22] and despite the rapid advances being made in medical care by the 1980s, surgery of this nature was still considered risky.

On February 12, Tullio went under the knife with Pat Liebel and Public Works Director Robert Waytenick taking charge of city business during his recovery. During the operation, doctors discovered the need to perform a quadruple bypass.[23]

As the city held its collective breath, Tullio emerged from the pro-

---

[19] Ibid.
[20] Ibid.
[21] "Heart Surgery Set for Tullio on Friday." Erie Times
    News. 5 Feb. 1982.
[22] Ibid.
[23] Ibid.

cedure in stable condition.[24] Just two days later, on Valentine's Day, in a rare moment of reflection, the once-strapping young football player acknowledged his own mortality.

"I did have my doubts that I would make it," he said. "I remember being wheeled into the operating room and saying, 'Hey, I don't want to do this, it's not too late to cancel, is it?'"

It was; the first thing he remembered after that was coming out of anesthesia.

"It's like being born again," said. Tullio "They've given me a new heart for Valentine's Day."[25]

But Tullio's new heart seemed made only to be broken when in July, the first calls for the complete removal of the Transitway Mall were heard.[26] Council President Robert Glowacki presented a proposal Tullio said that he would "consider,"[27] however, Tullio was dead-set against eradicating his one real plan to revitalize Erie's downtown.

By that time, however, the concept of the fully-enclosed suburban mall – the first of which appeared in Seattle in 1950 – had become popular across much of the United States, including Erie. According to Housing Authority of the City of Erie Executive Director John Horan, the historic role of downtowns like Erie's had begun to change from serving as the region's retail center to the region's cultural, recreational, and governmental center.[28]

While Tullio's embattled Transitway concept may have been a last-ditch effort to hold on to whatever downtown retail still existed, his civic center concept offered a more robust appeal to the cultural and recreational sensibilities of tourists and locals alike.

Instrumental to the development of that concept was Pennsylvania's Republican Governor Richard Thornburgh, who had allocated state funds[29] towards the Civic Center project and was, in 1982, up for reelection.

Tullio – a lifelong Democrat – endorsed Thornburg's candidacy "for

---

[24] "Tullio Stable During Surgery On His Heart." Erie Times News. 12 Feb. 1982.

[25] Grazier, Jack. "Thankful Tullio Happy it's Over." Erie Times News. 15 Feb. 1982.

[26] Miller, George. "Glowacki Wants $1 Million to End Downtown Mall." Erie Times News. 24 June 1982

[27] "Tullio Says He'll Consider Downtown Mall Changes." Erie Times News 1 July 1982.

[28] Horan, John. Author Interview with John Horan. 14 April 2015.

[29] Ibid.

what he's done for Erie"[30] and issued a statement to get out in front of any potential flak he might receive from his own party.

"I am more conscious of my responsibility as mayor of Erie than of any party role I might have served," Tullio said. "In my position of mayor, I represent all of our citizens, Democrats, Republicans, and Independents, and decisions I make for my city, I sincerely make in its best interest."[31]

Per Tullio, "One of the people in this state who has responded most readily to our requests for aid to Erie has been Gov. Dick Thornburgh. He has cooperated with us in every way we have asked him, and has provided us with additional monies for the Civic Center in the amount of $3.5 million."[32]

Again, Tullio's ability to turn enemies into friends had benefitted both himself and the city; during this time or just prior to it, Thornburgh was the most likely suspect as being behind the IRS' failed audit of Tullio years prior.

"I just had the sense at one point that one reason for it may have had to do with Thornburgh," said Tullio attorney Ed McKean. "At the time there was some thought that he was a political rival of Lou's because Lou had been mentioned in some quarters as a possible democratic candidate for governor. Whether that would've ever come to pass or not I don't know, but that would've made him Thornburgh's rival."[33]

With Tullio's endorsement – coming from a powerful Democrat in Pennsylvania's third-largest city – Thornburg won Erie County, and won reelection as governor with a very narrow margin. Also taking office in that election after a slim victory was the first enlisted Vietnam veteran to enter Congress – a local Republican attorney named Tom Ridge.[34]

As 1982 drew to a close, Tullio would need the help of Thornburgh and Ridge on the state and federal level more than ever. Another municipal budget was presented, with another deficit, another tax increase, and another water rate hike.[35]

Tullio, however, reminded taxpayers – and voters – of how his state

[30] Wellejus, Ed. "Surprise! Tullio Endorses Thornburgh." Erie Times News. 21 Oct. 1982.
[31] Ibid.
[32] Ibid.
[33] McKean, Edwin. Author interview with Edwin McKean. 23 Jan. 2015.
[34] "Thornburg Survives Strong Test." Erie Morning News. 3 Nov. 1982.
[35] Miller, George. "Tullio Presents Budget with 2.6 mill Tax Increase." Erie Times News. 30 Nov. 1982.

and national connections had benefitted them in the past.

"During my tenure in office as mayor of the city of Erie, my administration has made a concrete effort to actively seek monies from both the state and federal levels of government and bring them back to the city of Erie," he told reporter Ed Wellejus,[36] citing the $250 million he'd earned for Erie since 1965.

Putting it into perspective, that $250 million represented 448 mills[37] of real estate tax valuation; to raise comparable funds by taxing Erie homeowners would have required an additional 24 mills of taxation *every single year* over the 18 years Tullio had been in office. By comparison, real estate taxes had climbed to a rising total of 31 mills with the city's 1983 budget.

That summer, the ribbon was cut on one of the major cultural projects Tullio – without utilizing a single local dime[38] – bequeathed to Erie. Appropriately, that ribbon was cut by Thornburgh,[39] and also appropriately, that project was named after Tullio.

On June 7, 1983, the $15.3-million Erie Civic Human Resources Center complex – which included the Warner Theatre, as well as an exhibition hall on 10th and French streets – opened to the public; the centerpiece was the air-conditioned 7,500 seat multi-purpose arena, aptly named the Louis J. Tullio Convention Center.[40] On June 16, the Beach Boys christened the arena, which had already scheduled a summer's worth of concerts by popular acts of the time including Air Supply, Def Leppard, Gary Moore, Iron Maiden, Krokus, Linda Ronstadt, The Oak Ridge Boys, Sha Na Na, Rick Springfield, and James Taylor.[41]

Barry Gable, spokesman for the Cleveland-based Belkin Productions – the producers behind many of the shows – said that Erie would now be considered a "major market," while Tullio deemed it "a new beginning for Erie."

A new beginning was something Erie desperately needed; the trans-

---

[36] Wellejus, Ed. "Mayor's Job Will Never Be the Same Again." Erie Times News. 28 March 1983.
[37] Ibid.
[38] Tullio, Lou. "Tullio's Answer." Erie Times News. 9 Dec. 1982.
[39] "In Erie, a New Convention Era." Pennsylvania Economy Tabloid. August 1983.
[40] Ibid.
[41] Ibid.

formation of downtown from a regional retail hub to an entertainment and recreational destination was only beginning, but continuing budget problems – including *another* proposed 3.5 mill property tax increase for 1984 – made new sources of revenue critical.

Despite the tax increases, a poll conducted by Dr. Mark Iutcovich of the Keystone University Research Corporation showed more than 65 percent of voters giving Tullio – now in his 19th year as mayor – an "excellent" or "good" rating; only 21 percent thought his performance merely "fair" and just 10 percent thought him "poor."[42]

Right around the time that Tullio announced his intentions to wrest Erie's Bayfront from the tourism-smothering industrial nature of the area,[43] a 1984 study by geographer Robert M. Pierce of SUNY-Cortland rated Erie the 34th-best city (of 277 analyzed) in which to live,[44] even though Tullio's other major initiative – removal of the 19th Street railroad tracks – remained stalled.[45]

Astonishingly, some still believed he wasn't doing as good job as he could with the resources at his disposal; Tullio, who decided in November 1984 to seek yet another term, made the rounds and spoke with those who had been rumored as possible opponents in his reelection campaign.[46] A somewhat unorthodox move, Tullio's tour suggests that amidst his advancing age and recent bypass surgery, this would be his last term – one in which he wanted to go out on top, with as little opposition as possible.

The opposite occurred; the ever-oppositional Mario Bagnoni became the first to declare his intentions, in February 1985.

"I believe we have lost sight of what city government is supposed to be doing, which is providing the best available service at the lowest possible cost," Bagnoni said.[47]

Bagnoni did have a point in raising this issue; during this time in the city's history, escalating taxes made city services cost more and more each year; property taxes had *doubled* during Tullio's tenure and wa-

---

[42] Wellejus, Ed. "Poll Shows Tullio's Rating Just Keeps Climbing." Erie Times News. 6 Feb. 1984.

[43] Tullio, Lou. "Lower Bayfront Area Development Pushed." Erie Times News. 29 Jan. 1984: 6 - L.

[44] Benson, Mary. "Smile! Erie's 34th Best City in U.S." Erie Morning News. 25 April 1984.

[45] "A Solution to the 19th Street Tracks?" Erie Times News. 14 Dec. 1984.

[46] "Mayor Lou Tullio." Erie Times News. 27 Nov. 1984.

[47] "Bagnoni Opens Race for Mayor." Erie Morning News. 19 Feb. 1985

ter rates had increased eight-fold over the same period.[48] Bagnoni also claimed that Tullio's accomplishments were meager in relation to his failures, which, aside from taxes included the Transitway Mall and the 19th Street tracks.[49]

In March, the 40 year-old first-term City Controller – Chris Maras – joined Bagnoni and Tullio in the primary as well. Maras ran[50] on "youth," calling Tullio vulnerable.[51]

This situation must have been concerning for Tullio; Bagnoni had come rather close to defeating Tullio in 1981, despite Tullio being at the height of his popularity. With Maras in the mix, both Bagnoni and Tullio were bound to lose some votes – who would lose more was the real question, and for the second primary election in a row, Tullio once again faced a significant challenge to his power.

As the campaign shaped up, observers noted[52] Maras' weak effort; while Bagnoni said he didn't consider Maras a factor, Tullio campaigned like Bagnoni was the only man in the race.

"The campaign is going very, very well, even better than last time, because they really don't have issues," Tullio said, in a dig at Bagnoni. "We've accomplished so much more in the last four years."[53]

Voters agreed, and gave Tullio a somewhat comfortable margin of victory, considering the circumstances. Maras made a stronger-than expected showing at the polls, but it was nowhere near strong enough to give him a realistic chance of winning – his 5,536 votes were a distant third to Bagnoni's 8,820.[54]

Bagnoni again beat Tullio in the second ward, this time by 23 votes, but it would be the only ward he'd win. Tullio's 11,547 votes – including more than 4,400 in the Fifth Ward alone – were more than enough to push him over the top.

That fall, Tullio would go on to face his toughest Republican oppo-

---

[48] Ibid.
[49] Ibid.
[50] Miller, George. "Maras Runs for Mayor Nomination." Erie Daily Times. 4 March 1985.
[51] Miller, George. "Mayor Tullio: A Vulnerable Candidate?" Erie Times News. 13 Jan. 1985.
[52] Miller, George. "Mayor Candidates Ask: Where's Maras?" Erie Times News. 8 May 1985.
[53] Ibid.
[54] Miller, George. "Mayoral Contest Analyzed." Erie Times News. 24 May 1985.

nent since Mayor Williamson in the form of Anne Grunewald.

Grunewald wasted little time in going on the offensive against Tullio, starting with his recently prioritized Bayfront development plan – which included more recreational and residential opportunities than then existed – which she derided as "a massive assault on industry."[55]

Tullio's vision[56] for Bayfront revitalization targeted the well-known remaking of the Inner Harbor area of Baltimore, Maryland. Transformation of this urban waterscape – similar to Erie's – began in 1958 but took decades. By the late '60s, mixed-use and intelligently-planned buildings began sprouting up around green spaces and squares, converting an underutilized eyesore into an economic and aesthetic stimulus while also becoming hailed as one of the finest examples of such redevelopment in the country.

"We must preserve as much natural beauty of our bay as space allows," Grunewald said. "That's what brings tourists here, open spaces and free access."[57]

As incongruous as Grunewald's message was – for how, truly, does a beautiful Bayfront still include an asphalt shingle plant? – she revealed her pro-industry leanings by lamenting job loss and brain drain, as Tullio himself had done years before.[58]

"I am a mother. I am a grandmother. Why should you raise your children so they have to go somewhere else to raise a family?" complained Grunewald, citing her research that suggested that Erie had lost 20,000 jobs since Tullio took office.[59]

Tullio, armed with stats undermining Grunewald's claims and parsing through a stack of endorsements from local labor leaders said, "If they thought that there was a job problem, they wouldn't endorse me."[60]

Voters endorsed Tullio too; in typical Tullio fashion, he won every

[55] Thompson, Jim. "Grunewald Blasts Tullio Over Bayfront." Erie Times News. 25 Oct. 1985.
[56] "Erie Mayor Lou Tullio still running after five terms in office." The Gettysburg Times. 1 May 1985.
[57] Thompson, Jim. "Grunewald Blasts Tullio Over Bayfront." Erie Times News. 25 Oct. 1985.
[58] Allen, Liz. "Tullio, Grunewald Clash Over Jobless Rate Figures." Erie Morning News. 2 Nov. 1985.
[59] Ibid.
[60] Ibid.

ward – even the heavily-Republican Fourth Ward, where voters hadn't seen a real Republican since 1965. And yet again, his home ward – the fifth – provided the largest margin of any of them. When the dust settled, Tullio took home 15,847 votes to Grunewald's 10,919.

It was Tullio's second straight general election in which he failed to top his previous election's vote totals; despite his popularity, Tullio – now 69 years old – was facing increasing discontent from voters. "I feel it shows the people of Erie are very, very unhappy or I wouldn't have gotten the count I did," Grunewald said of her 4,928-vote deficit. "He's not as popular as he thinks he is. I don't think he has been for the normal taxpayer."[61]

Whether it was his age, or his health, or his slightly-yet-noticeably diminishing popularity, Tullio quickly announced that he'd just run his last campaign.

Sort of.

"This is it," Tullio said. "This is the last time... as long as no one talks me into it again."[62]

---

[61] Miller, George. "English in Split-Ticket Victory." Erie Daily Times. 6 Nov. 1985: 1.
[62] Ibid.

9

Not Fade Away

G IVEN THE CITY'S STATE OF AFFAIRS IN LATE 1985, IT PROBABLY WOULD
have taken a serious amount of talking to convince Lou Tullio to
run for a seventh term.

President Ronald Reagan – locked in what would ultimately be a
successful endeavor to outspend the Soviet Union into oblivion – had
drastically increased defense spending while simultaneously cutting the
tax rate for the nation's highest earners from 70 percent to 28 percent,
thus inflating the size of both the public debt and the federal budget
deficit to their highest levels since World War II.[1]

Social spending was an obvious casualty of Reagan's priorities; also
gone were the days of free-flowing federal aid to cities. Making matters
worse for recipients of discretionary spending, the *Gramm-Rudman-
Hollings Balanced Budget and Emergency Deficit Control Act of 1985* for
the first time created compulsory spending restrictions for appropria-
tions that exceeded expected spending.[2]

---

[1] Ippolito, Dennis. Why Budgets Matter: Budget Policy and American Politics. Penn
State Press, 2004.
[2] 99th Congress, S.1702, Pub.L. 99–177, title II. No. 99 Stat. 1038. 12 Dec. 1985.

As a result, before his sixth term even began, Tullio and the Erie City Council faced yet another budget deficit for 1986 – this time, $4 million – which, without higher revenues or lower spending, would require yet another property tax increase – in this case, almost 8 mills.[3]

To make matters worse, Governor Thornburgh refused to fund $30 million of a proposed $51 million package of improvements requested by the city. Among the casualties were the Erie Art Museum, the Warner Theatre, and the 19th street tracks initiative. Also cut – in a particularly painful blow to Tullio's Bayfront aspirations – were a proposed museum for Commodore Oliver Hazard Perry's flagship, the *Niagara*, and additional funding for the initial stages of Bayfront rejuvenation,[4] both of which may have languished due to a 1985 report[5] suggesting that not enough people lived close enough to Erie's Bayfront to make Baltimore-style redevelopment fiscally worthwhile.

This city's proposed budget for 1987 was little better, calling for a 5.5 mill increase to plug a $2.9 million deficit.[6]

Times were tough, to be sure – and Tullio's attempt to revitalize Erie's downtown retail core with the Transitway Mall wasn't helping.

On November 20, 1986, it was announced that the Transitway would soon open to regular, non-emergency vehicular traffic.[7] Removing it entirely was never really discussed, although the Transitway's death by a thousand cuts had been taking place for years now thanks to the protestations of various downtown business groups.[8]

Tullio – who'd worked so hard and held such high hopes for his novel, progressive, trendy development idea – was reluctant to admit defeat by discussing wholesale "removal" of the Transitway Mall, instead simply called it "widening," which, in reality, was tantamount to removal.

---

[3] Miller, George. "City Budget Has $4 Million Deficit." Erie Times News. 27 Nov. 1985.

[4] "Thornburgh vetoes funding for city, Bayfront projects." Erie Morning News. 11 July 1986.

[5] "Bayfront Development Recommendations Presented." Erie Times-News. 25 Aug. 1985.

[6] Miller, George. "Tullio Proposed Budget Stirs Controversy on Council." Erie Times News. 26 Nov. 1986.

[7] Miller, George. "Downtown Mall Will Open to Traffic." Erie Times News. 20 Nov. 1986.

[8] Pinksi, Jeff. "Tullio Eyes Funds to Widen State Street." Erie TImes News. 15 Nov. 1986.

"I'm working on it," he said of his attempt to obtain $1.2 million from the U.S. Department of Housing and Urban Development for the "widening."

Sam Sherman, owner of the Isaac Baker clothing store and president of an anti-Transitway group called Downtown Now said, "We're not saying by a long shot that getting rid of the mall is going to make the downtown what it once was. That may never happen. But the downtown can be revitalized and the mall is what's holding it up."[9]

"In my opinion, in retrospect it probably didn't matter a whole hell of a lot what we did downtown," said John Horan. "Retail was not coming back to downtown Erie. It took us a while to come to that conclusion, and meanwhile, the merchants who were still downtown were hoping that it would happen."

One instance, however, in Tullio's continuing effort to generate more revenue for the city proved that he could still squeeze money from the increasingly tight-fisted federal government; destined to help develop the Bayfront – which had been rezoned[10] from industrial to residential in June 1987 – a $4.5 million grant[11] from the U.S. Department of Housing and Urban Development would unofficially kick off an almost 30-year quest to reclaim Erie's scenic shore from a century's worth of industrial use.

Things were more or less how they'd always been in Erie – some ups, some downs – but for Tullio, it was obvious that most things were generally trending downwards.

Later that summer, Tullio – and all of Erie – would find out exactly where that trend would take them.

, , ,

"He got a request from someone for a donation to a party or a fundraiser or something, and he had a bar downstairs, so they asked him for some bottles of booze for the party," said Lou's brother John Tullio.[12] "So he went downstairs to get some bottles and put them into a case."

[9] Ibid.

[10] Miller, George. "Council Approves Bayfront Ordinance." Erie TImes News. 11 June 1987.

[11] "$4.5 Million Check Presented for Bayfront Project." Erie Times News. 8 June 1987.

[12] Tullio, John and Norma. Author interview with John and Norma Tullio. 15 Jan. 2015.

Lou then called his brother John on the phone, and asked him to come over to his house. When John arrived, he was greeted by a strange request.

"Come down a minute," Lou said to John.[13] "Would you mind carrying this upstairs for me?"

"He knew something was wrong," John said.[14] "He didn't know what it was, but that was the first indication. Here he was, this big strapping guy, a lot bigger than I am – he's over 6 foot, I'm under 5'10", and he's a lot huskier then I – and yet he's asking me to carry that upstairs. That was my first indication that there was something wrong."

Around the same time, Lou's daughter June Pintea noticed similarly uncharacteristic behavior from her father as they attended a backyard barbecue. While ascending a small hill on their way in to the party, halfway up, Lou paused.

"Oh gosh, I'm just so out of breath!" he said.

"Gee dad, that's not like you," June replied.

"Yeah, I know but I just feel like I'm really, really out of breath," he told her.

Not long after, an unrelated phone call to Pittsburgh Mayor Richard Caliguiri that had wound down into small talk about Tullio's health issues prompted Tullio to seek medical attention.[15]

"Hey, you sound like you have the same thing I have," said Caliguiri.[16]

The disease that would take Caliguiri's life in 1988 was amyloidosis.

Amyloidosis is a rare condition[17] that takes place when water-soluble proteins in the body, for some reason, begin to fold upon themselves abnormally, turning them into amyloids, which are no longer water-soluble. These proteins then begin to disrupt bodily functions by depositing themselves in various organs throughout the body.[18] Amyloidosis affects different people in different ways, often targeting the digestive tract, heart, kidneys, liver, nervous system, or spleen. It is incurable and eventually leads to death; the average life expectancy for someone diagnosed with it is 18 months.

---

[13] Ibid.
[14] Ibid.
[15] Ibid.
[16] Ibid.
[17] Mayo Foundation for Medical Education and Research. Amyloidosis. 1998. Retrieved 30 Oct. 2014.
[18] Ibid.

"In his case, it attacked his heart," John said.

John asked his own physician what that meant, exactly.

"You've seen an old leather wallet," the doctor told him. "Well, imagine when it gets real old and the leather gets sort of bent and it won't bend back – that's what's happening to his heart."[19]

In October 1987, Lou Tullio revealed his condition to the public.

"I do not want to leave office despite my health problems, as I am fully capable of discharging my duties as mayor. This disease in no way affects my mental capacity," he told reporters during a press conference. [20] "However, if I choose to remain, my doctors have informed me that I would have to drastically curtail my work and social schedule."

During that press conference, Tullio was asked why – after 22 years of serving the people of the City of Erie to the best of his ability – he did not just retire.[21]

"You can go home and fade away, too," said Tullio of his refusal to leave the playing field.[22]

His comment may have been a clever backhanded slap at whoever asked the question – possibly[23] Ed Mead himself – but Tullio's desire to not fade away was certainly not a joke.

As the laughter subsided, he continued.

"It's better to be carried out of City Hall than my home," he said.[24]

/ / /

On the last day of January in 1988, Lou – as he'd done many times before – penned an unofficial "state of the city" piece for the local paper; usually, he used his ink to both look back at the previous year's achievements as well as to look ahead at the coming year's opportunities.

Although he didn't mention his illness, the title of his article, "Future of Erie Exciting Despite Difficulties," said more than he probably knew.

---

[19] Tullio, John and Norma. Author interview with John and Norma Tullio. 15 Jan. 2015.

[20] Pinski, Jeff. "Tullio Vows to Stay in Office, Fight Disease." Erie Morning News. 12 Oct. 1987.

[21] Ibid.

[22] Pinski, Jeff. "Tullio Vows to Stay in Office, Fight Disease." Erie Morning News. 12 Oct. 1987.

[23] Tullio, John and Norma. Author interview with John and Norma Tullio. 15 Jan. 2015.

[24] Pinski, Jeff. "Tullio Vows to Stay in Office, Fight Disease." Erie Morning News. 12 Oct. 1987.

"This year will prove to be a very significant year for the community," he wrote. "Much has been written and spoken about the fiscal problems we face as a city, and we have worked diligently with city council to prepare what has proven to be the most difficult budget in my 22 years as mayor."[25]

The city's 1988 budget had again contained a 1-mill tax increase, even though "positive developments" were taking place throughout the city, including a gleaming new $14 million office complex at 100 State Street,[26] ongoing Bayfront renewal, and, yet again, another proposal to sell the city's water department to an independent authority.[27]

These developments, however, wouldn't make a significant impact in time to prevent another budget disaster in 1989; calling it "the worst financial crisis since I've been mayor," Tullio lamented the $1.5 million deficit and laid blame squarely on the "archaic system of political boundaries imposed by Harrisburg."[28]

The peculiarities of suburban boundaries that leave one building on one side of the street in one jurisdiction often leave another building on another side of the street in another jurisdiction – often a jurisdiction with a completely different tax rate.

"I would estimate that we lost over 60 percent of our commercial properties to Millcreek, Harborcreek, and Fairview," he said.

"These same [suburban] communities benefit from the tax-exempt facilities that are in Erie: the Civic Center, Warner Theatre, museum, zoo, hospitals, courthouse, colleges, public and Catholic Schools, churches, federal building, and courthouse. The city of Erie is the hub of the arts, cultural, and historical activities for the entire area. The city homeowners pay county taxes yet the county contributes nothing financially to the city."[29]

Amazingly, with a combination of clever cuts and creative revenue sourcing, 1989's budget required a tax increase of only one-half mill,[30] and as the last year of Tullio's mayoralty began, his annual "state of the

[25] Tullio, Lou. "Future of Erie Exciting Despite Difficulties." Erie Times News. 31 Jan 1988: 2 - M.

[26] Ibid.

[27] Pinski, Jeff. "Water Authority Proposed." Erie Morning News. 8 July 1988.

[28] Wellejus, Ed. "Tullio Says City is in Big Trouble.: Erie Times News. 10 Nov. 1988.

[29] Ibid.

[30] Miller, George. "Erie Raises Tax One-Half Mill." Erie Times News. 23 Dec. 1988.

city story" again revealed in its title more than Tullio probably knew: "City Continues to Plan for Future, Meet Challenges."[31]

🔳 🔳 🔳

While Tullio was busy meeting challenges, others in government were actively planning for *their* futures.

Carl "Skip" Cannavino – nephew to both Tullio and Mike Cannavino – was the first to announce his campaign for mayor, in November 1988.[32] Cannavino had served as deputy city treasurer for 15 years under 40-year veteran treasurer Francis Haggerty, and then served as city treasurer for five terms of his own.[33]

Cannavino would soon be joined in the Democratic Municipal Mayoral Primary by a who's who of Erie politics at the time – including Bob Brabender, Pat Cappabianca, Chris Maras, Joyce Savocchio, and Tullio's preferred candidate, longtime assistant Pat Liebel.

Aging Councilmen Brabender and Cappabianca had both run against Tullio before; although Liebel obviously hadn't, all three of them had waited their entire lives to occupy the mayor's seat on the fifth floor of City Hall, especially knowing that while Tullio still stood on the field, doing so was a near-impossibility.

For them the primary couldn't come soon enough – likewise for Maras, the also-ran, and Savocchio, the first woman ever elected to city council.

Much of Erie probably felt the same; beginning in January 1989, a series of hospitalizations would call into question Tullio's ability to effectively lead the city he'd helmed for 23 years.

Tullio was hospitalized[34] with a viral infection in early January; once he was discharged in mid-January, he embarked on a much-needed California vacation with his wife that would keep him out of Erie until March.

Right around the time that he left, calls for his resignation began to emanate from a familiar source – Councilman Mario Bagnoni.[35]

[31] Tullio, Lou. "City Continues to Plan for Future, Meet Challenges." Erie Times News. 29 Jan. 1989: 8 - L.
[32] Miller, George. "Cannavino Becomes First Candidate for Mayor." Erie Times News. 29 Nov. 1988.
[33] Cannavino, Skip. Author interview with Skip Cannavino. 8 Jan. 2015.
[34] Miller, George. "Tullio Reported to be Feeling Better." Erie Times News. 9 Jan. 1989.
[35] Pinski, Jeff. "Bagnoni Call for Tullio to Quit Rebuffed by Colleagues." Erie Morning News. 12 Jan. 1989.

"I pray for him and his recovery every day," Bagnoni said. "But if he can't do the job full-time, he ought to think about getting out and getting someone in here who can do the job full-time."[36]

City Council President Bob Brabender – a longtime foe of Tullio's – jumped to Tullio's defense, stating that after a visit with Tullio in the hospital, he felt Tullio was still capable of operating as Mayor.[37]

After a quiet February, Tullio returned from California in early March, and was promptly hospitalized again for a fluid buildup in his lungs.[38] After he was released, in what would become Tullio's new normal, the same condition would send him right back to the hospital on April 15.[39]

The first real indicator that Bagnoni may have been right came on the heels of Tullio's most recent hospitalization. On April 18, the *Erie Times-News* reported that Councilman Pat Cappabianca was claiming that the city had lost $1.27 million in reimbursement from the state for the city's underfunded pension funds by not filing the proper forms by the proper date.[40] Cappabianca's claims were substantiated, although claims of a cover-up about the fumble – probably pointed at Liebel and levelled by Republican City Controller (and future Congressman) Phil English – were not.[41]

Erie would still receive more than $2 million in reimbursement from the state for the pension funds, but it's difficult to imagine something like this happening with a vibrant, vital Tullio still doing what he'd done so well for so long – talking state and federal leaders into opening their wallets for Erie. The loss of $1.27 million represented 3 mills of property tax valuation at the time.

Memorial Day 1989 would again find Tullio in the hospital, prompting him to finally address his capabilities and assure the public that he was still in control of major decision-making.[42]

"I'm getting stronger each day," he said.

[36] Ibid.
[37] Ibid.
[38] "Tullio's Condition Listed as Good." Erie Morning News. 21 Mar. 1989.
[39] "Tullio Still in Hospital for Rest, Treatment." Erie Morning News. 18 Apr. 1989.
[40] Miller, George. "City Loses $1.27 Million Refund by not FIling Forms on Deadline." Erie Times News. 18 Apr. 1989.
[41] Ibid.
[42] "Tullio Says He'll Make All Major Decisions." Erie Morning News. 7 June 1989.

Also growing stronger were certain local politicos who, for the first time in a long time, actually had a shot at becoming mayor.

The field of candidates – Maras, Savocchio, Cannavino, Cappabianca, Liebel, and Brabender – offered several interesting choices for voters; personalities and ethnicities aside, the choice was effectively one of old versus new, of continuing Tullio's governing style and policies or rejecting them.

Liebel was the obvious choice for those wishing to perpetuate the policies of Tullio; she'd worked with Tullio in a professional capacity for his entire mayoral tenure, and was probably the most qualified candidate in terms of experience. Also well-qualified – because of their combined 36 years on council – were Brabender and Cappabianca, who, while not directly associated with Tullio, were certainly associated with the type of old-school Erie politics that Tullio was. The same went for Cannavino, who'd been in city government longer than Tullio had.

The relatively young Chris Maras represented the "youth" movement; inexperienced and less connected to Tullio than others, Maras offered voters a clean break from the Tullio years, despite being largely unproven and a previous loser to Tullio (and Bagnoni) in the 1985 mayoral primary.

Sitting right in the middle of that spectrum was Joyce Savocchio – after eight years on council, she wasn't inexperienced, but she also wasn't as close to the Tullio era as Brabender, Cannavino, and Cappabianca. Neither insider nor outsider, neither old-school nor new, she occupied a comfortable middling zone in the minds of voters, who rewarded her with victory by a margin of less than two percent.

Bringing up the rear was Bob Brabender, who failed to win a single ward and collected 2,511 votes – or about 9.9 percent – in a heavily-fragmented primary. Liebel, who had spent more than $100,000 on her Tullio-backed campaign, also won no wards and came in just ahead of Brabender with 3,190 votes, good for 12.6 percent. The second tier of candidates – Cappabianca and Maras – both came in at 16 percent, with Maras surprisingly winning the first and second wards.

Savocchio had been badly outspent[43] by Liebel during the campaign, however, the real contest was between Savocchio and Cannavino.

---

[43] Corbran, Paul. "Liebel Outspends Mayoral Opponents." Erie Times News. 21 June 1989.

Cannavino was competitive with Savocchio in the Maras-led First and Second Wards, and lost slight ground to her in the Third and Fourth Wards. Savocchio beat Cannavino in the Sixth Ward – her home turf – by just 95 votes, but as had happened with Tullio so many times before, the Fifth Ward had weighed in on who was to lead the city for the seventh mayoral election in a row.

Tullio's traditional stronghold went for Savocchio 2,122 to 1,968, ensuring that Savocchio would, in the end, earn just enough votes to again leave a Cannavino frustratingly short of their mayoral aspirations. Skip's 5,408 votes – good for 21.37 percent of the total – were simply not enough; Savocchio's 23.14 percent – 5,855 votes – would leave her lined up to face retired city water department chief and Republican Mayoral Candidate Stanley Prazer in the fall.

As Tullio sat on the sidelines watching the first mayoral primary he hadn't run in since 1961, his health continued to deteriorate; another persistent aggravation – the municipal budget – again sparked calls for Tullio, who by his own admission was still making all major decisions, to appoint an acting mayor.

During preliminary budget talks for the city's 1990 fiscal year in July 1989, a projected $3.5 million deficit again loomed; when Brabender was disappointed with the extent of proposed cuts by Tullio, he lashed out.

"Lou Tullio is no longer a functioning mayor," Brabender complained.[44] "We wish Lou still had the reigns, but he does not."

Brabender's remark may have been born of frustration over yet another ugly budget, but just days after he made it, an editorial in the *Erie Times-News* lent credence to the theory that Brabender wasn't simply using Tullio's illness as an excuse to call for his removal:

With Sadness, We Suggest Tullio Retire

Because we feel Erie needs day-to-day leadership, particularly in the upcoming city budget talks, we at the Times Publishing Company have come to a difficult decision: We think it is time for Mayor Tullio to make another sacrifice for the city he loves. We think the mayor ought to retire, leaving the arena of battle to oth-

---

[44] Pinski, Jeff. "Brabender Calls for Acting Mayor to Replace Tullio." Erie Morning News. 27 July 1989.

er gladiators. Because the political process continues whether the circumstances, the last few months have not been kind to Mayor Tullio. Politics and political infighting continue and the mayor has been unable to respond. Impressions that a more vital Tullio would have demolished without a second's thought have been allowed to remain and fester. It is all so unfair and the only way to end it is for the mayor to make a complete break, to retire and let someone else deal with the day-to-day grievances inevitable in the city this size. But more than that, Erie needs hands-on leadership in the budget crisis, leadership of the type Tullio, because of his battle with the incurable disease amyloidosis, is no longer able to give. A mayor who can give the city his full attention is necessary. For the long view, for history, Tullio need have no fear. His reputation as one of the greats of Erie history, as the only mayor to be elected to six consecutive terms, will endure...[45]

The elegantly-worded suggestion by the editorial board of the *Times* continued on respectfully and delicately – a noble gesture by an oft-adversarial publication that had frequently criticized Tullio during its century-long mission to comfort the afflicted and afflict the comfortable.

Notably, this editorial would also showcase the proclivity of Erieites to play out their most controversial conversations on the pulpy pages of their city's most hallowed publication. The very next day, a story in the *Times* showed[46] support for Tullio's decision to remain in charge; both Savocchio and Prazer agreed that only the new mayor would be able to bring Erie the clean break it needed.

By early September, a proposal was floated – by Bagnoni – to appoint[47] City Councilman Brian Dougherty as acting mayor. Tullio, however, remained in control despite now working out of his living room, surrounded by family.

"Grace was still working," Lou's Daughter June Pintea said.[48] "She

[45] "With Sadness, We Suggest Tullio Retire." Erie Times News. 30 July 1989.
[46] Thompson, Jim. "Mayor Candidates, Party Chiefs Say Tullio Should Stay in Office." Erie Times News. 31 July 1989.
[47] Miller, George. "Dougherty Proposed as Acting Mayor." Erie Times News 6 Sept. 1989.
[48] Pintea, June. Author interview with June Pintea, 22 Jan. 2015.

ran a successful real estate business, so she would go back to New Jersey one week out of every month, and when she would leave, I would come over."

June and others would care for him, spending afternoons reminiscing and evenings disregarding Grace's strict dietary instructions.

"Grace had this little list about things he cannot have," said June.[49] "Once she left, we decided he's going to have them if he wants them! So we did that. We did not tell her, though."

What Tullio – a lifelong gourmand – wanted most of all, was bratwurst.[50]

♪ ♪ ♪

Two events that took place in October 1989 provided a rare and serendipitous culmination to the circular nature of Lou Tullio's journey from son of immigrants to confidant of presidents.

On Sunday, October 1, 1989, Tullio was well enough to attend Gannon's first home football game since 1950; he'd been at their last one, too, serving as head coach, until budget constraints forced the termination of the program.[51]

The game – a 22-to-0 loss for the Golden Knights – must have dredged up lots of old memories for Tullio, who in 1950 was a 34 year-old father-of-three who had only been back in his home town for three years after a more than a decade spent at college in Massachusetts, at war in the Pacific, and at work as a milkman.

Just two weeks later, more memories floated to the surface for Tullio as the Erie City Council voted five to two in favor of a proposal to once and for all sell the city's water department to an independent authority.[52]

Strangely, an authority had already been created, way back in the initial rounds of Tullio's decades-long effort to rid the city of the water department; they held neither meetings nor assets, and received neither salaries nor customer payments. They merely existed, for 23 years.

On October 22, Tullio made his first appearance at City Hall since May 2.[53]

---

[49] Ibid.
[50] Ibid.
[51] "Coach Returns." Erie Morning News. 2 Oct. 1989.
[52] "Council Votes 5-2 for Water Authority." Erie Morning News. 19 Oct. 1989.
[53] "League of Cities Honors Tullio." Erie Morning News. 22 Oct. 1989.

"I feel weak today," he told reporters, who told him he looked good.

"I always look good," he said.[54]

The occasion of his visit was to attend a ceremony hosted by the Pennsylvania League of Cities, who were to honor him by planting a tree in Perry Square. As good as he may have looked on that brisk fall day, Tullio watched the dedication from his car.

* * *

A few weeks later, Erie would learn the name of its next elected mayor; perhaps much of Erie had already known that name when Joyce Savocchio edged out a difficult Democratic Municipal Mayoral Primary field in May, but November's General Election would make it official.

Merely a technicality at this point – as the traditional Democrat versus Republican paradigm had broken down in the early 1960s in Erie and other similar urban environments due to a demographic shift that now included women, Jews, African-Americans, Hispanics, and many other non-traditional constituency groups in the ruling coalition – November's General Election was a tremendous success for Savocchio, who defeated Stanley Prazer in Tullioesque manner; she won all six wards, earned more than one-third of her margin from the Fifth Ward alone, and racked up 22,956 votes to Prazer's 10,080.

Savocchio wouldn't be inaugurated until January 1990, however, in early-November 1989 there was still work to be done, and a budget to finish; just after the election, as movers packed up the amazing amount of memorabilia that coated nearly every available surface in Tullio's office,[55] concerns again shifted to the ancient seasonal rituals in Erie – filling the potholes, policing the streets, presiding over renewal, staving off decline, and plugging the budget holes.

"We're getting to be involved heavily in the budget from here on out," said Pat Liebel on November 9, reflecting on boxes full of photos, tokens, totems, and other assorted official miscellanea one might expect the mayor of a major American city would collect over the course of nearly a quarter century in office. "That's where we want to put our complete concentration without worrying about moving out."[56]

The next day, Lou Tullio resigned.[57]

---

[54] Ibid.
[55] "Time Comes to Move Out of Mayor's Office." Erie Morning News. 9 Nov. 1989.
[56] Ibid.
[57] "Erie Mayor Resigns Due to Rare Illness." Indianapolis Star. 11 Nov. 1989.

10

A Real Erie Guy

April in the Commonwealth of Pennsylvania is always a time of great change; it is a month of transition, during which the wintry weather of months past continues to make occasional and unwelcomed appearances, but the summery weather of months yet to come begins to dominate more and more, day by day.

Stretching more than 8,713 days, Lou Tullio's time as mayor reflected the influence of several eras in American politics; he had one foot in the roaring '20s and one in the depression-era '30s, his heart in the postwar economic boom of the '50s and '60s, and his head in the mediocre '70s and '80s.

But much like that fateful phone call to The Garden State Park Racetrack in Cherry Hill, New Jersey on October 22, 1965 – the one that propelled Lou into higher office – April 17, 1990 would bring another phone call that would also involve Lou, Pat Liebel, and "higher office."

"You better come back up," voice on the other end said.

It was Lou's wife, Grace.[1]

---

[1] Liebel, Patricia. Author interview with Patricia Liebel. 7 Jan. 2015.

"By the time I got back," said Pat Liebel, "why, he was gone." She'd just returned home from visiting Lou at his home. "I really think he was ready to go," she said. "He couldn't do the things that he used to do. He was an active man, he was always on the phone constantly – I mean, his whole life, he was on the go – and I think to be hampered by something that you just can't do anything about, because his heart was just getting weaker and weaker, he knew that it was time."

Liebel – who'd lost to Savocchio in the primary but was appointed Acting Mayor of the City of Erie by Lou upon his resignation – had, in her seven-week tenure, helped deliver a $35.3 million balanced budget with only a quarter-mill tax increase for 1990 that was, fittingly, the last official act in which Lou had had his hand.[2]

It is at this point in history where Louis Joseph Tullio turns from just an unsophisticated-yet-effective local politician into one of the most heavily mythologized politicians in Erie's 200-plus year history.

Mentioning Lou around Erie elicits a wide spectrum of opinions; older generations of Erieites all have something to say about him, as do younger. Anyone born in Erie from the early '30s to the early '80s recalls him and for some, he was the only mayor they'd ever known.

Sometimes, what they say about Lou is part of his mythology.

He was crooked. He took suitcases full of money. He was mafia. He did this. He did that.

But in his day, everything Tullio did was not only acceptable, but expected – and completely legal. Handing out patronage jobs was, at the time, how one maintained a hold on political power, and how things got done in a city of Erie's size.

Sure, things had changed by the end of Lou's reign, but when Tullio, and Cannavino, and those before them held court, they were made from the mold of George Washington Plunkitt – a New York State Legislator and Tammany Hall politician who preserved for posterity his practical philosophies on "honest graft"[3] in *Plunkitt of Tammany Hall* much as

---

[2] Pinski, Jeff. "Erie City Council Passes 1990 Budget." Erie Morning News. 21 Dec. 1989.

[3] Plunkitt of Tammany Hall: A Series of Very Plain Talks on Very Practical Politics, Delivered by Ex-senator George Washington Plunkitt, the Tammany Philosopher, from His Rostrum — the New York County Court House Bootblack Stand. New York: Penguin Publishing Group, 1995.

Niccolò Machiavelli preserved his theories[4] on governance in *The Prince* centuries earlier.

Dishonest graft, held Plunkitt, was working only for one's own personal interests; honest graft was working for the interests of one's own personal interests alongside the interests of one's government and one's party.

Lou – and those like him, including Chicago's Mayor Richard J. Daley – were most interested in enriching their power bases, not their wallets.

His attorney Ed McKean endured a 5-year IRS audit with him and was privy to all of Lou's financial dealings at that time; as McKean himself opined, if anyone was in a position to know if Lou was taking money, it was McKean.

"Lou never took a nickel in his life," he said.[5]

Tullio's daughter June Pintea – who had long ago married one of Lou's most frequent critics, *Times* Managing Editor Larie Pintea – would also have learned (while his estate was being settled) if her father was personally enriching himself at the expense of taxpayers.

"Did you find the suitcases full of money?" her husband Larie would joke.

"If he had a suitcase full of money," June replied, "I'm apparently not looking around very well."[6]

June elaborated.

"If he had a sizable fortune, I think I would've known," she said. "Grace was a millionaire in her own right – she was a very successful businesswoman, she was a very astute businesswoman… So if he had a fortune I sure as heck never saw it… Grace got the house, all the proceeds went to her, so I don't know. I don't see a great fortune. I really don't, but then again, who knows. I don't know. I would like to think not, because his grandchildren should have benefited from that."

Trumping the suppositions of both Lou's attorney McKean and his daughter June, the most authoritative source on the matter – the IRS – had vindicated Lou after a politically motivated and groundless audit. Not only that, but if McKean's recollection is correct, the IRS –

---

[4] Machiavelli, Niccolò, Harvey C. Mansfield (Translator). The Prince. Chicago: University of Chicago Press, 1998.

[5] McKean, Edwin. Author interview with Edwin McKean. 23 Jan. 2015.

[6] Pintea, June. Author interview with June Pintea, 22 Jan. 2015

the most relentless and single-minded collection agency on the planet – ended up issuing "Lucky Lou" a tax refund.

Other similarly unsupported mythology surrounding Lou includes the usual vagaries levelled at public figures in Erie, especially a supposed connection to organized crime.

Based on the work of Dominick DiPaulo and Jeff Pinski in *The Unholy Murder of Ash Wednesday*, during Lou's time there were really only two "made" guys in Erie,[7] and Lou was not one of them.

According to off-record sources, the "mafia" in Erie was no more or less a constituency group than any other, however, their influence on city government – and on Lou himself – was minimal to nonexistent.

Near the end of his service, Lou reflected on a career spent in the spotlight.

"The scrutiny, the rumors, the lack of privacy are all very difficult," he said. "You have to expect that if you hold public office."[8]

Sometimes, however, what older and younger generations of Erieites have to say about Lou actually stems from fact.

Dealing with budget troubles seemed to be the hallmark of his tenure as mayor. When state and federal funds flowed freely, Lou – a natural politician with a knack for telling one where to go in such a fashion as to make them look forward to the trip – earned for his beloved Erie far more than her fair share, and for that, the entire region owes him a debt of gratitude.

He helped spend it, too; all those patronage jobs that kept him in power all those years cost taxpayers money, which is, again, why that sort of thing doesn't happen as much anymore; such preferential hiring leads, in the long run, to an assortment of societal ills categorized roughly as "-isms" – nepotism and bossism.

In Erie, it also led to loose purse-strings and little regard for rainy days. As spending during what Fred Rush called "the good days" continued to rise, when the rain did come, often the only umbrella was to raise taxes or find other ways to acquire income.

Sadly, risky development schemes like the Transitway Mall – which, at times, made the cure worse than the disease – were never more than

[7] DiPaulo, Dominick D. as told to Jeff Pinski. The Unholy Murder of Ash Wednesday. Erie, PA: Global Roman Publishing, 2014.
[8] Dahlkemper, Mary Ellen. "Were You Born a Mayor?" Erie & Chautauqua Magazine 1989: 51.

tiny buttresses against a raging sea of globalism, computers, and robotics; emerging concepts like these were making traditional American manufacturing less competitive, and towns like Erie somewhat vulnerable.

All of Lou's efforts in office were not for naught, however. Over the course of 23 years, he became the city's first *true* strong mayor, serving as an exemplar for leadership that is used to measure Erie's mayors even today. He became the first Italian mayor in a city where Italian culture runs a century deep and 39 miles wide, and resolved to make that city a "metropolitan community of major national importance."

While attempting to do so, he fought through a 90-year old debate about the status of the city's water department only to see it resolved on his deathbed. He engaged in a decades-long fight to remove the 19th street railroad tracks, which, at the time of his death, still carried freight both east and west, as they'd done for 108 years prior. He was the first Erie mayor to grapple with the debilitating and self-inflicted civic inferiority complex reinforced by sarcastic sayings like, "dreary Erie," and "the mistake on the lake." He unwisely challenged an incumbent congressman and was humbled.

But he did have a hand in creating what is known today as "Celebrate Erie," the city's largest annual festival that sprang from the failure of the city to sponsor a citywide fireworks display in America's Bicentennial year. He survived suburbanization and the death of downtown and the IRS audit. He laid the groundwork for the arena that would one day bear his name for a time, saved the Warner Theatre, and expanded Erie's port. He also dealt – on a daily basis – with a myriad of important issues like affordable housing, the sales and display of pornography in the city, allegations of police corruption, labor strikes, and pollution.

Late in life, he heard new voices in Council Chambers, and even as his own health deteriorated, he imagined – in what would be his last and most visionary desire – a Bayfront reinvigorated.

Fact or myth, everyone certainly has something to say about Lou; the tenure of this American Tullius was bookended by death – on one end, by that of Mike Cannavino and on the other end, his own. His time in office spanned from Jefferson Airplane to Starship; from "White Rabbit" to "We Built This City,"[9] and until the rise of fellow Erieite Tom

---

[9] Scalise, Todd. Author interview with Todd Scalise. 14 May 2015.

Ridge in the late 1990s, he was the most significant historical figure in Erie since Oliver Hazard Perry in the 1820s.

"People still remember him," said Liebel. "Good and bad, they still remember him."[10]

Liebel was recently in a grocery store checkout line when the man behind her struck up a conversation.

"Are you Pat Liebel?" he asked.

"Yes, I am." Liebel responded.

"Well, I want you to know that I never voted for Lou Tullio one time! I thought he was a real S.O.B. and I never voted for him once! But I like you. And you know what? I sure wish he was here now to run the city."[11]

Joyce Savocchio can also testify to how Lou was remembered, even outside Erie.

"I always use one example," she said.[12] "When I became mayor, we'd go to the U.S. Conference of Mayors and that. Some of the old mayors were still around when I came in, and they would say, 'Mayor! Mayor! You followed Lou Tullio!'"

Perhaps the most significant way he is remembered is in the physical imprint that he left on his city, like King Richard the Builder had on his; looking deeper, however, it is clear that the most important means by which he has influenced Erie's bright future is not in in his works but in the deeds of his proud past – Lou served as a mentor to and example for generations of leaders in this city.

One young prodigy he mentored was Dr. William P. Garvey, who first met Lou when he was a student at Gannon in the 1950s. Garvey went on to be a lifelong confidant of and friend to Lou, and, on April 20, 1990, eulogized[13] him at St. Peter's Cathedral.

In doing so, Garvey gave the textbook definition of what it means to be a real Erie guy:

[10] Liebel, Patricia. Author interview with Patricia Liebel. 7 Jan. 2015.

[11] Ibid.

[12] Savocchio, Joyce. Author Interview with Joyce Savocchio. 20 Apr. 2015.

[13] Garvey, Dr. William P. "Mayor Louis J. Tullio: An Erie Guy - His Last Hurrah." Erie, Pa., 20 Apr. 1990.

You don't have to be ethnic, but it helps. You have a sense of the place and its nuances and its Midwestern warmth and friendliness toward strangers. You have a special feeling for the bay and Presque Isle. You brag about Erie sunsets and complain about Erie weather. You shake your head at the heated politics that seem to continually grip the city, but are quick to voice your own opinion and put forth your own ideas when you don't agree. You attend countless dinners, testimonials, and celebrations in the clubs and bars that abound everywhere. You deplore the city's small-town mentality, but love the fact that you can be anywhere in 20 minutes without the traffic jams of the 'big city.'

You wonder about the city's future but admit it's a great place to raise a family. You laugh at Erie jokes but resent them for secretly, deep down, 'Erie guys' really love their city, although some consider it bad form to show it.

Real Erie guys are all too few – and now, one fewer.

BIBLIOGRAPHY

Chapter 1 - Tell Them I Want to Run

[1] Liebel, Patricia. Author interview with Patricia Liebel. 7 Jan. 2015.
[2] Strauss, Robert. "The Track Has Run Its Course". 29 Apr. 2001. New York Times. Accessed 27 Feb. 2015.
[3] Baker, Jeanne. Italian Politics. Mercyhurst University, 1970.
[4] Liebel, Patricia. Author interview with Patricia Liebel. 7 Jan. 2015.

Chapter 2 - To Finish Out on Top

[1] "Mike A. Cannavino obituary." Erie Morning News. 25 Oct. 1965: sec. B p. 2.
[2] Foust, Kyle. "Why Lou Tullio: How Erie's Most Powerful Mayor Came to Power." Journal of Erie Studies (2003): 57-75.
[3] Ibid.
[4] Cannavino, Skip. Author Interview with Skip Cannavino. 8 Jan. 2015.
[5] Erie Hall of Fame. Mike Cannavino. Accessed 27 Feb. 2015.
[6] Cannavino, Skip. Author Interview with Skip Cannavino. 8 Jan. 2015.
[7] Liebel, Patricia. Author interview with Patricia Liebel. 7 Jan. 2015.
[8] Ibid.
[9] Ibid.
[10] Ibid.
[11] Ibid.
[12] Foust, Kyle. "Why Lou Tullio: How Erie's Most Powerful Mayor Came to Power." Journal of Erie Studies 32 no. 2, 2003: 57-75.
[13] Ibid.
[14] Ibid.
[15] Ibid.
[16] Garvey, William P. PhD. The Ethnic Factor in Erie Politics. PhD. diss., University of Pittsburgh, 1973.
[17] Sennett, William C. The 1961 Erie Mayoral Election. Journal of Erie Studies 32 no. 2, 2003: 29-46.
[18] Ibid.
[19] Ibid.
[20] Ibid.
[21] Ibid.
[22] Ibid.
[23] Ibid.
[24] Ibid.
[25] Brodsky, Alyn. The Great Mayor. New York: St. Martin's Press, 2003 (75).
[26] Foust, Kyle. "Why Lou Tullio: How Erie's Most Powerful Mayor Came to Power." Journal of Erie Studies 32 no. 2, 2003: 57-75.

27 Ibid.
28 Ibid.
29 Garvey, William P. PhD. The Ethnic Factor in Erie Politics. PhD. diss., University of Pittsburgh, 1973.
30 Foust, Kyle. "Why Lou Tullio: How Erie's Most Powerful Mayor Came to Power." Journal of Erie Studies 32 no. 2, 2003: 57-75.
31 Garvey, William P. PhD. The Ethnic Factor in Erie Politics. PhD. diss., University of Pittsburgh, 1973.
32 Sennett, William C. The 1961 Erie Mayoral Election. Journal of Erie Studies 32 no. 2, 2003 29-46.
33 Garvey, William P. PhD. The Ethnic Factor in Erie Politics. PhD. diss., University of Pittsburgh, 1973.
34 Ibid.
35 Spartacus Educational. Immigration Peak Years. n.d. 31 Jan. 2015.
36 Garvey, William P. PhD. The Ethnic Factor in Erie Politics. PhD. diss., University of Pittsburgh, 1973.
37 Spartacus Educational. Immigration Peak Years. n.d. 31 Jan. 2015.
38 Garvey, William P. PhD. The Ethnic Factor in Erie Politics. PhD. diss., University of Pittsburgh, 1973.
39 Tullio, John and Norma. Author interview with John and Norma Tullio. 15 Jan. 2015.
40 Tullio. Accessed 9 Nov. 2014. <http://www.spokenhere.com/tag/tullio>.
41 Tullio, John and Norma. Author interview with John and Norma Tullio. 15 Jan. 2015.
42 Works Progress Administration. WPA Workers Handbook. 1936. Accessed 30 Mar. 2015.
43 Howard, Pat. "Erieites express their views of Lou Tullio as man, mayor." Erie Daily Times. 17 April 1990: sec. B, p. 1.
44 Tullio, John and Norma. Author interview with John and Norma Tullio. 15 Jan. 2015.
45 Ibid.
46 Cuneo, Pat. "The Sportsman: A look at how athletic coaching, competition forged the legend." Erie Morning News. 18 Apr. 1990: [special section] p. 11.
47 Ibid.
48 Tullio, John and Norma. Author interview with John and Norma Tullio. 15 Jan. 2015.
49 Cuneo, Pat. "The Sportsman: A look at how athletic coaching, competition forged the legend." Erie Morning News. 18 Apr. 1990: [special section] p. 11.
50 Pinski, Jeff. "Area mourns loss of Lou Tullio." Erie Morning News. 18 Apr. 1990: sec. 1 p. 1.
51 Tullio, John and Norma. Author interview with John and Norma Tullio. 15 Jan. 2015.
52 Cappabianca, Pat. Author interview with Pat Cappabianca. 5 Jan. 2015.
53 Pintea, June. Author interview with June Pintea. 22 Jan. 2015.
54 Ibid.

55 Ibid.
56 Ibid.
57 Ibid.
58 Ibid.
59 Tullio, John and Norma. Author interview with John and Norma Tullio. 15 Jan. 2015.
60 Cuneo, Pat. "The Sportsman: A look at how athletic coaching, competition forged the legend." Erie Morning News. 18 Apr. 1990: [special section] p. 11.
61 Pintea, June. Author interview with June Pintea. 22 Jan. 2015.
62 Ibid.
63 Ibid.
64 Ibid.
65 Cuneo, Pat. "The Sportsman: A look at how athletic coaching, competition forged the legend." Erie Morning News. 18 Apr. 1990: [special section] p. 11.
66 Garvey, William P. PhD. The Ethnic Factor in Erie Politics. PhD. diss., University of Pittsburgh, 1973.
67 Cuneo, Pat. "The Sportsman: A look at how athletic coaching, competition forged the legend." Erie Morning News. 18 Apr. 1990: [special section] p. 11.
68 Ibid.
69 Foust, Kyle. "Why Lou Tullio: How Erie's Most Powerful Mayor Came to Power." Journal of Erie Studies 32 no. 2, 2003: 57-75.
70 Ibid.
71 Ibid.
72 Rogowski, Bill. "Party Committeeman Make Vote Unanimous." Erie Morning News. 25 Oct. 1965: sec. 1 p. 1.

Chapter 3 - Lucky Lou

1 Minegar, Garth. City Mourns Mike. Erie Times News. Oct. 24, 1965, sec. 1, p. 1.
2 Ibid.
3 Ibid.
4 Liebel, Patricia. Author interview with Patricia Liebel. 7 Jan. 2015.
5 Ibid.
6 Rush, Fred. Author interview with Fred Rush. 14 Jan. 2015.
7 Liebel, Patricia. Author interview with Patricia Liebel. 7 Jan. 2015.
8 Wellejus, Ed. Erie: Chronicle of a Great Lakes City. Woodland Hills, CA: Windsor Publications, 1980.
9 Garvey, William P. PhD. The Ethnic Factor in Erie Politics. PhD. diss, University of Pittsburgh, 1973.
10 Ibid.
11 Ibid.
12 Cannavino, Skip. Author interview with Skip Cannavino. 8 Jan 2015.
13 Foust, Kyle. "Why Lou Tullio: How Erie's Most Powerful Mayor Came to Power." Journal of Erie Studies, vol. 32, no. 2 (2003): 57-75.
14 Ibid.

[15] Ibid.

[16] Cannavino, Skip. Author interview with Skip Cannavino. 8 Jan 2015.

[17] Ibid.

[18] Pintea, June. Author interview with June Pintea. 22 Jan. 2015.

[19] Garvey, William P. PhD. The Ethnic Factor in Erie Politics. PhD. diss, University of Pittsburgh, 1973.

[20] Ibid.

[21] Ibid.

[22] Foust, Kyle. "Why Lou Tullio: How Erie's Most Powerful Mayor Came to Power." Journal of Erie Studies 32, no. 2, 2003: 57-75.

[23] Ibid.

[24] Garvey, William P. PhD. The Ethnic Factor in Erie Politics. PhD. diss, University of Pittsburgh, 1973.

[25] Cannavino, Skip. Author interview with Skip Cannavino. 8 Jan 2015.

[26] Foust, Kyle. "Why Lou Tullio: How Erie's Most Powerful Mayor Came to Power." Journal of Erie Studies 32 no. 2, 2003: 57-75.

[27] Cannavino, Skip. Author interview with Skip Cannavino. 8 Jan 2015.

[28] Ibid.

[29] Minegar, Mike. "City Mourns Mike." Erie Times News. 24 Oct. 1965: sec. 1, p. 1.

[30] Ibid.

[31] Foust, Kyle. "Why Lou Tullio: How Erie's Most Powerful Mayor Came to Power." Journal of Erie Studies, vol. 32, no. 2 (2003): 57-75.

[32] Ibid.

[33] Ibid.

[34] "Mike A. Cannavino obituary." Erie Morning News. 25 Oct. 1965: sec. B, p. 2.

[35] Foust, Kyle. "Why Lou Tullio: How Erie's Most Powerful Mayor Came to Power." Journal of Erie Studies, vol. 32, no. 2 (2003): 57-75.

[36] Ibid.

[37] Cannavino, Skip. Author interview with Skip Cannavino. 8 Jan 2015.

[38] Foust, Kyle. "Why Lou Tullio: How Erie's Most Powerful Mayor Came to Power." Journal of Erie Studies 32 no. 2, 2003: 57-75.

[39] Ibid.

[40] Ibid.

[41] Ibid.

[42] Ibid.

[43] Garvey, William P. PhD. The Ethnic Factor in Erie Politics. PhD. diss, University of Pittsburgh, 1973.

[44] Ibid.

[45] Ibid.

[46] Ibid.

[47] Ibid.

Chapter 4 - Lessons and Losses

[1] City's 45th Mayor. Erie Daily Times. 3 Jan. 1966.

[2] Ibid.

154 *Lou Tullio: A Real Erie Guy*

3 Ibid.
4 Ibid.
5 Garvey, William P. PhD. The Ethnic Factor in Erie Politics. PhD. diss., University of Pittsburgh, 1973.
6 Tullio, Mayor Confer. Erie Daily Times. 17 Nov. 1965: sec. 1 p. 3.
7 Garvey, William P. PhD. The Ethnic Factor in Erie Politics. PhD. diss., University of Pittsburgh, 1973.
8 Ibid.
9 Ibid.
10 Ibid.
11 Ibid.
12 Ibid.
13 Tullio, Mayor Confer. Erie Daily Times. 17 Nov. 1965: sec. 1 p. 3.
14 City's 1965 Spending Down. Erie Times News. 9 Jan. 1966.
15 Cappabianca, Pat. Author interview with Pat Cappabianca. 5 Jan. 2015
16 Green, Cornell. "You Ought to Know: Pat Cappabianca." The Erie Reader, 2 Dec. 2011.
17 Cappabianca, Pat. Author interview with Pat Cappabianca. 5 Jan. 2015
18 Ibid.
19 Garvey, William P. PhD. The Ethnic Factor in Erie Politics. PhD. diss., University of Pittsburgh, 1973.
20 Liebel, Patricia. Author interview with Patricia Liebel. 7 Jan. 2015.
21 Ibid.
22 Ibid.
23 Ibid.
24 Lyon, Debbi. Coach Lou Tullio and Erie Vets 1948 Football at Erie Stadium. 11 Jul. 2012. 9 Mar. 2015.
25 Flowers, Kevin. Longtime City Leader Robie Dies at 82. 8 July 2006. Erie Times News. Accessed 14 Mar. 2015.
26 McKean, Edwin. Author interview with Edwin McKean. 23 Jan. 2015.
27 Pintea, June. Author interview with June Pintea. 22 Jan. 2015.
28 Liebel, Patricia. Author interview with Patricia Liebel. 7 Jan. 2015.
29 Ibid.
30 Pintea, June. Author interview with June Pintea. 22 Jan. 2015.
31 McKean, Edwin. Author interview with Edwin McKean. 23 Jan. 2015.
32 Ibid.
33 Ibid.
34 Liebel, Patricia. Author interview with Patricia Liebel. 7 Jan. 2015.
35 Ibid.
36 Ostrowski, Mark. "The Beginning of a Regime: An Analysis of Louis J. Tullio's Governing Style, 1961 - 1969." 1991.
37 Ibid.
38 Liebel, Patricia. Author interview with Patricia Liebel. 7 Jan. 2015.
39 Ibid.
40 Cannavino, Skip. Author interview with Skip Cannavino. 8 Jan.

2015.
[41] Liebel, Patricia. Author interview with Patricia Liebel. 7 Jan. 2015.
[42] Ibid.
[43] Cappabianca, Pat. Author interview with Pat Cappabianca. 5 Jan. 2015.
[44] Garvey, William P. PhD. The Ethnic Factor in Erie Politics. PhD. diss., University of Pittsburgh, 1973.
[45] Ibid.
[46] Rush, Fred. Author interview with Fred Rush. 13 Jan. 2015.
[47] Garvey, William P. PhD. The Ethnic Factor in Erie Politics. PhD. diss., University of Pittsburgh, 1973.
[48] Ostrowski, Mark. "The Beginning of a Regime: An Analysis of Louis J. Tullio's Governing Style, 1961 - 1969." 1991.
[49] National Advisory Commission on Civil Disorders. "Report of the National Advisory Commission on Civil Disorders." 1968.
[50] Ostrowski, Mark. "The Beginning of a Regime: An Analysis of Louis J. Tullio's Governing Style, 1961 - 1969." 1991.
[51] Ibid.
[52] Rush, Fred. Author interview with Fred Rush. 13 Jan. 2015.
[53] Ibid.
[54] Ostrowski, Mark. "The Beginning of a Regime: An Analysis of Louis J. Tullio's Governing Style, 1961 - 1969." 1991.
[55] Ibid.
[56] Pintea, June. Author interview with June Pintea. 22 Jan. 2015.
[57] Tullio, John and Norma. Author interview with John and Norma Tullio. 15 Jan. 2015.
[58] Nies III, Thomas G. A Study of the Brabender Family and their Role in Erie Political History. Mercyurst College. Erie, Pa., 1999.
[59] Pintea, June. Author interview with June Pintea. 22 Jan. 2015.
[60] Ibid.
[61] Garvey, William P. PhD. The Ethnic Factor in Erie Politics. PhD. diss., University of Pittsburgh, 1973.
[62] Sundberg, Peggy. "Tullio's Win - Tears of Joy and Sadness." Erie Morning News. 5 Nov. 1969: sec. 1, p. 1.
[63] Sundberg, Peggy. "Brabender Concedes Early." Erie Morning News. 5 Nov. 1969: sec. 1, p.1.
[64] Ibid.
[65] Ibid.
[66] Ibid.
[67] Pintea, June. Author interview with June Pintea, 22 Jan. 2015.
[68] "Erie's First Lady Dies After Lingering Illness." Erie Morning News. 7 Nov. 1969.

Chapter 5 - Dear and Beloved Enemies

[1] Ostrowski, Mark. "The Beginning of a Regime: An Analysis of Louis J. Tullio's Governing Style, 1961 - 1969." 1991.
[2] Pintea, June. Author interview with June Pintea. 22 Jan. 2015.
[3] Ostrowski, Mark. "The Beginning of a Regime: An Analysis of Louis

J. Tullio's Governing Style, 1961 - 1969." 1991.
4 Sundberg, Peggy. "Brabender Concedes Early." Erie Morning News
5 Nov. 1969: sec. 1, p.1.
5 "City's 45th Mayor." Erie Daily Times. 3 Jan. 1966.
6 Rush, Fred. Author interview with Fred Rush. 13 January 2015.
7 Ibid.
8 Ibid.
9 Ibid.
10 Cuneo, Kevin. "Ed Mead, Erie newspaper icon dies at 88." Erie
Times News. 12 Mar. 2015.
11 Rush, Fred. Author interview with Fred Rush. 13 January 2015.
12 Hunt, D. Bradford. Encyclopedia of Chicago. 2005. Retrieved 31
Jan. 2015.
13 Ostrowski, Mark. "The Beginning of a Regime: An Analysis of Louis
J. Tullio's Governing Style, 1961 - 1969." 1991.
14 Ibid.
15 Horan, John. Author Interview with John Horan. 14 April 2015.
16 Tullio, Lou. "Many Projects Planned for City." Erie Times News. 23
Jan. 1972: V 2.
17 "Tullio Discloses City Could End Year in Red." Erie Times News. 9
Nov. 1969: IIIG.
18 "City Spent $7.6 Million in 7 Months." Erie Times News. 14 Aug.
1970: IIIG 144.
19 National Advisory Commission on Civil Disorders. "Report of the
National Advisory Commission on Civil Disorders." 1968.
20 City-data.com. http://www.City-Data.com. n.d. 13 Feb. 2015.
<http://www.city-data.com/township/Millcreek-Erie-PA.html>.
21 Graney, Grossman, Colosimo and Associates Inc. Erie County
Demographic Study. Erie County, Pa., Jan. 2003.
22 United States Census Bureau. Ninteenth U.S. Census. Washington:
GPO, 1970.
23 "City Spending Borrowed Money." Erie Times News. 5 Sept. 1970:
IIIG 152.
24 Kermisch, Amos. "City Council Defeats, 4-3, Water Works
Transfer." Erie Daily Times. 16 Dec. 1970: A-1.
25 Cappabianca, Pat. Author interview with Pat Cappabianca. 5 Jan. 2015.
26 Ibid.
27 Ibid.
28 Voters Reject Water Department Plan, Walczak, Orlando Lead
Council Tickets. Erie Morning News. 18 May 1971: 1.
29 $1 Million Deficit Looms for City. Erie Times News. 7 July 1971:
IV-I 105.
30 City Spending Up A Bit, Despite Austerity Plan. Erie Morning
News. 28 Jun. 1971: B-1.
31 11-14 Mill Tax Increas Faces Property Owners. Erie Times News.
23 Aug. 1971: IV - I 123.
32 Federal Aid Helped Limit Possible Tax Hike In City. Erie Morning
News. 26 Nov. 1971: C-5.

[33] Council Celebrate Eve with One Mill Tax Increase. Erie Times News. 1 Jan. 1972: IV-I 192.

[34] Seminar Explains Transitway Plan. Erie Morning News. 21 Nov. 1969: 13.

[35] Matthews, Ed. Odds & Ends. Erie Times News. 5 Apr. 1970: C-2.

[36] Hearing Scheduled on Transitway. Erie Times News. 4 Apr. 1973: VI 109.

[37] Plans Unveiled for Millcreek Mall. Erie Times News. 26 Jun. 1973: VII 41.

[38] Quick Mall Start Seen. Erie Times News. 4 Aug. 1973.

[39] State Street to Close Monday. Erie Times News. 8 Aug. 1973: VII 87.

[40] Guerriero, John. 19th Street Tracks Laid to Rest. Erie Times News. 15 May 2002. Retrieved 1 April 2015.

[41] Tullio Seeks Funds For Track Removal. Erie Morning News. 5 May 1970.

[42] Ibid.

[43] Ibid.

[44] Erie Western Pennsylvania Port Authority. n.d. 2 Apr. 2015. <http://www.porterie.org/about/>.

[45] Ibid.

[46] "Tullio Asks Council OK Port Authority." Erie Times News. 23 Mar. 1973.

[47] Mayor Proposes Port Compromise. Erie Morning News. 29 Mar. 1973.

[48] Ibid.

[49] Thompson, Jim. $19 Million Port Authority Plans Viewed. Erie Times News. 6 May 1973.

[50] Pintea, June. Author interview with June Pintea. 22 Jan. 2015.

[51] NorthJersey.com. Obituary: Grace Gunster Tullio, 95. 14 Feb. 2014. Retrieved 28 Jan. 2015.

[52] Postnuptual Party Honors Mayor, Mrs. Tullio. Erie Times News. 11 Aug 1971.

[53] Tullio, John and Norma. Author interview with John and Norma Tullio. 15 Jan. 2015.

[54] Grace Tullio: First Lady. Erie Morning News. 23 Nov. 1988.

[55] Ibid.

[56] Ibid.

[57] Liebel, Patricia. Author interview with Patricia Liebel. 7 Jan. 2015.

[58] Wellejus, Ed. Author interview with Ed Wellejus. 13 Jan. 2015.

[59] Obituary: Mario S. Bagnoni. 6 Aug. 2005. Retrieved 22 Jan. 2015.

[60] National Music Museum. 24 Apr. 2014. Retrieved 11 Mar. 2015.

[61] Pallatella, Ed. Mario Bagnoni has only one opponent left. Himself. Erie Times News. 21 May 2003. Retrieved 11 Mar. 2015.

[62] Ibid.

[63] Cappabianca, Pat. Author interview with Pat Cappabianca. 5 Jan. 2015.

[64] Wellejus, Ed. "Tullio and Bagnoni." Erie Times News. 19 Mar. 1972.

[65] Tullio, John and Norma. Author interview with John and Norma

Tullio. 15 Jan. 2015.
[66] McKean, Edwin. Author interview with Edwin McKean. 23 Jan. 2015.
[67] Liebel, Patricia. Author interview with Patricia Liebel. 7 Jan. 2015.
[68] McKean, Edwin. Author interview with Edwin McKean. 23 Jan. 2015.
[69] Liebel, Patricia. Author interview with Patricia Liebel. 7 Jan. 2015.
[70] Wellejus, Ed. Author interview with Ed Wellejus. 13 Jan. 2015
[71] Pinksi, Jeff. Bagnoni Considering Mayoral Try. Erie Morning News 13 Sept. 1972.
[72] Walczak Thinking of Mayoral Run. Erie Morning News 14 Sept. 1972.
[73] Pinski, Jeff. Bags, Walczak Touted to Head Tullio Drive. Erie Times News. 12 Jan. 1973.
[74] Tullio Returns Harkins Blast. Erie Morning News. 11 Aug. 1972.
[75] Democratic Candidates for Mayor Speak Out. Erie Morning News. 15 May 1973.
[76] Here Come Da Mayors. Erie Times News. 1971 15 June.
[77] Thompson, Jim. Tullio Scores Landslide: Third 4-Year Term Possible for Mayor. Erie Morning New.s 16 May 1973: 1.
[78] Cappabianca, Pat. Author interview with Pat Cappabianca. 5 Jan. 2015.

Chapter 6 - Strange Days

[1] Cappabianca, Pat. Author interview with Pat Cappabianca. 5 Jan. 2015.
[2] Foht, Richard. Author Interview with Richard Foht. 18 Apr. 2015.
[3] Wellejus, Ed. Tullio for Governor? Erie Times News. 30 Sept. 1973.
[4] Foht, Richard. Author Interview with Richard Foht. 18 Apr. 2015.
[5] Ibid.
[6] McKean, Edwin. Author interview with Edwin McKean. 23 Jan. 2015.
[7] Ibid.
[8] Foht, Richard. Author Interview with Richard Foht. 18 Apr. 2015.
[9] Ibid.
[10] Ibid.
[11] Exceptions Filed to Mall Ruling. Erie Morning News. 10 July 1973.
[12] Tullio Calls Foht "Karnes' Puppet." Erie Morning News. 14 Sept. 1973.
[13] Foht, Richard. Author Interview with Richard Foht. 18 Apr. 2015.
[14] Ibid.
[15] Ibid.
[16] Ibid.
[17] Ibid.
[18] Ibid.
[19] Liebel, Patricia. Author interview with Patricia Liebel. 7 Jan. 2015.
[20] McKean, Edwin. Author interview with Edwin McKean. 23 Jan. 2015.
[21] Ibid.

[22] Ibid.
[23] Ibid.
[24] Liebel, Patricia. Author interview with Patricia Liebel. 7 Jan. 2015.
[25] McKean, Edwin. Author interview with Edwin McKean. 23 Jan. 2015.
[26] Thompson, Jim. Tullio Inaugurated to Third Term; Vows 'Performance Administration. Erie Times News. 7 Jan. 1974.
[27] Bill Cosby, Arbors to Appear at Downtown Mall Fete. Erie Times News. 8 Sept. 1974.
[28] Tullio, Ford Meet Today. Erie Times News. 10 July 1975.
[29] Thompson, Jim, and Dick Garcia. Tullio, Hilinski Enter '75 With Matching Headaches. Erie Times News. 1 Jan. 1975.
[30] www.cbsnews.com. 2002. 16 Apr. 2015. <http://www.cbsnews.com/news/tv-guide-names-top-50-shows/>
[31] Thompson, Jim. Lamary Quip Angers Erieites. Erie Times News. 14 Apr. 1973.
[32] Ibid.
[33] Horan, John. Author Interview with John Horan. 14 April 2015.
[34] Ibid.
[35] Erie Wins All-America Award As Top U.S. City. Erie Daily Times. 3 Apr. 1973: 1.
[36] The National Civic League. www.nationalcivicleague.org/2014. 29 Apr. 2015. <http://www.nationalcivicleague.org/>.
[37] Ibid.
[38] Thompson, Jim. Lamary Quip Angers Erieites. Erie Times News. 14 Apr. 1973.
[39] Tullio Nominated to US Mayors Post. Erie Times News. 14 June 1971.
[40] The Unites States Conference of Mayors. About USCM. 2015. <http://www.usmayors.org/meetmayors/mayorsatglance.asp>.
[41] Biographical Dictionary of the United States Congress. Vigorito, Joseph Phillip. n.d. 19 Mar. 2015.
[42] Ray, Alex. Hired Gun: A Political Odyssey. Lanham, Maryland: University Press of America, 2008.
[43] Tullio Announcement Seen. Erie Times News. 15 Jan. 1976.
[44] Brown, Warren. Vigorito Gets Job Brushoff From Capitol. The Pittsburgh Press. 26 June 1977: A-28.
[45] Wellejus, Ed. Tullio for Congress? Erie Times News. 10 Mar. 1975.
[46] Wellejus, Ed. Fourth Term for Tullio? Erie Times News. 1 June 1975.
[47] Tullio Announcement Seen. Erie Times News 15 Jan. 1976.
[48] Ibid.
[49] Ibid.
[50] Garvey, William. What Really Happened? A Political Analysis of the Tullio-Vigorito Democratic Primary. Erie Today Aug. 1976: 28-9, 41.
[51] Vigorito Trounces Tullio. Erie Times News. 28 Apr. 1976.
[52] Garvey, William. What Really Happened? A Political Analysis of the Tullio-Vigorito Democratic Primary. Erie Today Aug. 1976: 28-9, 41.
[53] Vigorito Trounces Tullio. Erie Times News. 28 Apr. 1976.

54 Garvey, William. What Really Happened? A Political Analysis of the Tullio-Vigorito Democratic Primary. Erie Today Aug. 1976: 28-9, 41.
55 Rush, Fred. Author interview with Fred Rush. 13 January 2015.

Chapter 7 - Simple Orchestrations

1 Quiet Bicentennial Sparks Controversy. Erie Morning News. 14 July 1976.
2 Horan, John. Author Interview with John Horan. 14 April 2015.
3 Quiet Bicentennial Sparks Controversy. Erie Morning News. 14 July 1976.
4 Horan, John. Author Interview with John Horan. 14 April 2015.
5 Ibid.
6 Grazier, Jack. Good Year For Lots of Things, Including Controversy. Erie Times News. 28 December 1976: 12-B.
7 Grazier, Jack. Track Removal Almost Certain, Tullio Believes. Erie Times News. 9 Mar. 1977.
8 Horan, John. Author Interview with John Horan. 14 April 2015.
9 Foht Quits Politics. Erie Times News. 18 May 1977.
10 Foht, Richard. Author Interview with Richard Foht. 18 Apr. 2015.
11 Ibid.
12 Mayor Plans Erieland Celebration. Erie Times News. 7 July 1977.
13 Tullio Defends Pension Against Doutt's Claims. Erie Times News. 20 Oct. 1977: 22-a.
14 Foht Quits Politics. Erie Times News. 18 May 1977.
15 McKinney, Bill. Tullio to Present '78 Budget to Council. Erie Morning News. 30 Nov. 1977.
16 Foht, Richard. Author Interview with Richard Foht. 18 Apr. 2015.
17 McKean, Edwin. Author interview with Edwin McKean. 23 Jan. 2015.
18 Ibid.
19 Liebel, Patricia. Author interview with Patricia Liebel. 7 Jan. 2015.
20 McKean, Edwin. Author interview with Edwin McKean. 23 Jan. 2015.
21 Ibid.
22 Ibid.
23 Ibid.
24 Ibid.
25 Ibid.
26 Tullio, Lou. A Very Productive Year for Erie. Erie Times News. 28 Jan. 1979: 12 G.
27 Ibid.
28 City Real Estate Tax Increased by Two Mills in 1979 Budget. Erie Times News. 27 Dec. 1978: 1.
29 Mayoral Priorities Picked. Erie Morning News. 12 June 1979.
30 Bagnoni, Tullio Clash Over Water. Erie Morning News. 21 Aug. 1979.
31 Ibid.
32 Ibid.

[33] Ibid.

[34] Wellejus, Ed. Author interview with Ed Wellejus. 13 Jan. 2015.

[35] Cappabianca, Pat. Author interview with Pat Cappabianca. 5 Jan. 2015.

[36] McKean, Edwin. Author interview with Edwin McKean. 23 Jan. 2015.

[37] Ibid.

[38] Tullio Has 'Mixed Emotions.' Erie Morning News. 15 Jan. 1981.

[39] Ibid.

[40] Pasquale, Tony. Chief Defends Police, Raps Bagnoni for Criticism. Erie Morning News. 23 April 1981.

[41] Tullio Has 'Mixed Emotions.' Erie Morning News. 15 Jan. 1981.

[42] Tullio, Lou. Projects Keep Erie Moving. Erie Times News. 25 Jan. 1981: 2-L.

[43] Groundbreaking Galore! Erie Morning News. 21 April 1981.

[44] Bagnoni Letter Praises Mayor Tullio. Erie Times News. 6 May 1981.

[45] Ibid.

[46] McKinney, Bill. "Tullio Wins Dem Primary After Hard-Fought Battle." Erie Morning News. 20 May 1981: 1.

[47] Miller, George. Cannavino Becomes First Candidate for Mayor. Erie Times News. 29 Nov. 1988.

[48] Ibid.

[49] Ibid.

[50] Sanfilippo, Vicki. Lynch Already at Work; Johnson Gracious Loser; Tullio Beats Hammer 3 to 1. Erie Daily Times. 4 Nov. 1981: 1.

Chapter 8 - A New beginning

[1] Garvey, William P. PhD. The Ethnic Factor in Erie Politics. University of Pittsburgh, 1973.

[2] Savocchio, Joyce. Author Interview with Joyce Savocchio. 20 Apr. 2015.

[3] Ibid.

[4] Ibid.

[5] Ibid.

[6] Ibid.

[7] Ibid.

[8] Ibid.

[9] Ibid.

[10] Ibid.

[11] Ibid.

[12] Ibid.

[13] Ibid.

[14] Liebel, Patricia. Author interview with Patricia Liebel. 7 Jan. 2015.

[15] Savocchio, Joyce. Author Interview with Joyce Savocchio. 20 Apr. 2015.

[16] Council Passes City Budget in 4 Minutes. Erie Times News. 2 Jan. 1982.

[17] Ibid.

[18] Tullio Enters Historic Fifth Term as Mayor. Erie Morning News. 5 Jan. 1982.

[19] Ibid.

[20] Ibid.

[21] Heart Surgery Set for Tullio on Friday. Erie Times News. 5 Feb. 1982.

[22] Ibid.

[23] Ibid.

[24] Tullio Stable During Surgery On His Heart. Erie Times News. 12 Feb. 1982.

[25] Grazier, Jack. Thankful Tullio Happy it's Over. Erie Times News. 15 Feb. 1982.

[26] Miller, George. Glowacki Wants $1 Million to End Downtown Mall. Erie Times News. 24 June 1982

[27] Tullio Says He'll Consider Downtown Mall Changes. Erie Times News 1 July 1982.

[28] Horan, John. Author Interview with John Horan. 14 April 2015.

[29] Ibid.

[30] Wellejus, Ed. Surprise! Tullio Endorses Thornburgh. Erie Times News. 21 Oct. 1982.

[31] Ibid.

[32] Ibid.

[33] McKean, Edwin. Author interview with Edwin McKean. 23 Jan. 2015.

[34] Thornburg Survives Strong Test. Erie Morning News. 3 Nov. 1982.

[35] Miller, George. Tullio Presents Budget with 2.6 mill Tax Increase. Erie Times News. 30 Nov. 1982.

[36] Wellejus, Ed. Mayor's Job Will Never Be the Same Again. Erie Times News. 28 March 1983.

[37] Ibid.

[38] Tullio, Lou. Tullio's Answer. Erie Times News. 9 Dec. 1982.

[39] In Erie, a New Convention Era. Pennsylvania Economy Tabloid. August 1983.

[40] Ibid.

[41] Ibid.

[42] Wellejus, Ed. Poll Shows Tullio's Rating Just Keeps Climbing. Erie Times News. 6 Feb. 1984.

[43] Tullio, Lou. Lower Bayfront Area Development Pushed. Erie Times News. 29 Jan. 1984: 6 - L.

[44] Benson, Mary. Smile! Erie's 34th Best City in U.S. Erie Morning News. 25 April 1984.

[45] A Solution to the 19th Street Tracks? Erie Times News. 14 Dec. 1984.

[46] Mayor Lou Tullio. Erie Times News. 27 Nov. 1984.

[47] Bagnoni Opens Race for Mayor. Erie Morning News. 19 Feb. 1985

[48] Ibid.

[49] Ibid.

[50] Miller, George. Maras Runs for Mayor Nomination. Erie Daily Times. 4 March 1985.

[51] Miller, George. Mayor Tullio: A Vulnerable Candidate? Erie Times News. 13 Jan. 1985.
[52] Miller, George. Mayor Candidates Ask: Where's Maras? Erie Times News. 8 May 1985.
[53] Ibid.
[54] Miller, George. Mayoral Contest Analyzed. Erie Times News. 24 May 1985.
[55] Thompson, Jim. Grunewald Blasts Tullio Over Bayfront. Erie Times News. 25 Oct. 1985.
[56] Erie Mayor Lou Tullio still running after five terms in office. The Gettysburg Times. 1 May 1985.
[57] Thompson, Jim. Grunewald Blasts Tullio Over Bayfront. Erie Times News. 25 Oct. 1985.
[58] Allen, Liz. Tullio, Grunewald Clash Over Jobless Rate Figures. Erie Morning News. 2 Nov. 1985.
[59] Ibid.
[60] Ibid.
[61] Miller, George. English in Split-Ticket Victory. Erie Daily Times. 6 Nov. 1985: 1.
[62] Ibid.

Chapter 9 - Not Fade Away

[1] Ippolito, Dennis. Why Budgets Matter: Budget Policy and American Politics. Penn State Press, 2004.
[2] 99th Congress, S.1702, Pub.L. 99–177, title II. No. 99 Stat. 1038. 12 Dec. 1985.
[3] Miller, George. City Budget Has $4 Million Deficit. Erie Times News. 27 Nov. 1985.
[4] Thornburgh vetoes funding for city, Bayfront projects. Erie Morning News. 11 July 1986.
[5] Bayfront Development Recommendations Presented. Erie Times News. 25 Aug. 1985.
[6] Miller, George. Tullio Proposed Budget Stirs Controversy on Council. Erie Times News. 26 Nov. 1986.
[7] Miller, George. Downtown Mall Will Open to Traffic. Erie Times News. 20 Nov. 1986.
[8] Pinksi, Jeff. Tullio Eyes Funds to Widen State Street. Erie Times News. 15 Nov. 1986.
[9] Ibid.
[10] Miller, George. Council Approves Bayfront Ordinance. Erie Times News. 11 June 1987.
[11] $4.5 Million Check Presented for Bayfront Project. Erie Times News. 8 June 1987.
[12] Tullio, John and Norma. Author interview with John and Norma Tullio. 15 Jan. 2015.
[13] Ibid.
[14] Ibid.
[15] Ibid.

[16] Ibid.

[17] Mayo Foundation for Medical Education and Research. Amyloidosis. 1998. Retrieved 30 Oct. 2014.

[18] Ibid.

[19] Tullio, John and Norma. Author interview with John and Norma Tullio. 15 Jan. 2015.

[20] Pinski, Jeff. Tullio Vows to Stay in Office, Fight Disease. Erie Morning News. 12 Oct. 1987.

[21] Ibid.

[22] Pinski, Jeff. Tullio Vows to Stay in Office, Fight Disease. Erie Morning News. 12 Oct. 1987.

[23] Tullio, John and Norma. Author interview with John and Norma Tullio. 15 Jan. 2015.

[24] Pinski, Jeff. Tullio Vows to Stay in Office, Fight Disease. Erie Morning News. 12 Oct. 1987.

[25] Tullio, Lou. Future of Erie Exciting Despite Difficulties. Erie Times News. 31 Jan 1988: 2 - M.

[26] Ibid.

[27] Pinski, Jeff. Water Authority Proposed. Erie Morning News. 8 July 1988.

[28] Wellejus, Ed. Tullio Says City is in Big Trouble.: Erie Times News. 10 Nov. 1988.

[29] Ibid.

[30] Miller, George. Erie Raises Tax One-Half Mill. Erie Times News. 23 Dec. 1988.

[31] Tullio, Lou. City Continues to Plan for Future, Meet Challenges. Erie Times News. 29 Jan. 1989: 8 - L.

[32] Miller, George. Cannavino Becomes First Candidate for Mayor. Erie Times News. 29 Nov. 1988.

[33] Cannavino, Skip. Author interview with Skip Cannavino. 8 Jan. 2015.

[34] Miller, George. Tullio Reported to be Feeling Better. Erie Times News. 9 Jan. 1989.

[35] Pinski, Jeff. Bagnoni Call for Tullio to Quit Rebuffed by Colleagues. Erie Morning News. 12 Jan. 1989.

[36] Ibid.

[37] Ibid.

[38] Tullio's Condition Listed as Good. Erie Morning News. 21 Mar. 1989.

[39] Tullio Still in Hospital for Rest, Treatment. Erie Morning News. 18 Apr. 1989.

[40] Miller, George. City Loses $1.27 Million Refund by not Filing Forms on Deadline. Erie Times News. 18 Apr. 1989.

[41] Ibid.

[42] Tullio Says He'll Make All Major Decisions. Erie Morning News. 7 June 1989.

[43] Corbran, Paul. Liebel Outspends Mayoral Opponents. Erie Times News. 21 June 1989.

[44] Pinski, Jeff. Brabender Calls for Acting Mayor to Replace Tullio.

Erie Morning News. 27 July 1989.

[45] With Sadness, We Suggest Tullio Retire. Erie Times News. 30 July 1989.

[46] Thompson, Jim. Mayor Candidates, Party Chiefs Say Tullio Should Stay in Office. Erie TImes News. 31 July 1989.

[47] Miller, George. "Dougherty Proposed as Acting Mayor." Erie Times News 6 Sept. 1989.

[48] Pintea, June. Author interview with June Pintea, 22 Jan. 2015.

[49] Ibid.

[50] Ibid.

[51] Coach Returns. Erie Morning News. 2 Oct. 1989.

[52] Council Votes 5-2 for Water Authority. Erie Morning News. 19 Oct. 1989.

[53] League of Cities Honors Tullio. Erie Morning News. 22 Oct. 1989.

[54] Ibid.

[55] Time Comes to Move Out of Mayor's Office. Erie Morning News. 9 Nov. 1989.

[56] Ibid.

[57] Erie Mayor Resigns Due to Rare Illness. Indianapolis Star. 11 Nov. 1989.

Chapter 10 - A Real Erie Guy

[1] Liebel, Patricia. Author interview with Patricia Liebel. 7 Jan. 2015.

[2] Pinski, Jeff. Erie City Council Passes 1990 Budget. Erie Morning News. 21 Dec. 1989.

[3] Plunkitt of Tammany Hall: A Series of Very Plain Talks on Very Practical Politics, Delivered by Ex-senator George Washington Plunkitt, the Tammany Philosopher, from His Rostrum ó the New York County Court House Bootblack Stand. New York: Penguin Publishing Group, 1995.

[4] Machiavelli, Niccolo, Harvey C. Mansfield (Translator). The Prince. Chicago: University of Chicago Press, 1998.

[5] McKean, Edwin. Author interview with Edwin McKean. 23 Jan. 2015.

[6] Pintea, June. Author interview with June Pintea, 22 Jan. 2015

[7] DiPaulo, Dominick D. as told to Jeff Pinski. The Unholy Murder of Ash Wednesday. Erie, PA: Global Roman Publishing, 2014.

[8] Dahlkemper, Mary Ellen. Were You Born a Mayor? Erie & Chautauqua Magazine 1989: 51.

[9] Scalise, Todd. Author interview with Todd Scalise. 14 May 2015.

[10] Liebel, Patricia. Author interview with Patricia Liebel. 7 Jan. 2015.

[11] Ibid.

[12] Savocchio, Joyce. Author Interview with Joyce Savocchio. 20 Apr. 2015.

[13] Garvey, Dr. William P. "Mayor Louis J. Tullio: An Erie Guy - His Last Hurrah." Erie, Pa., 20 Apr. 1990.

Index

INDEX

U.S. Rail Association 104

V

Vallecorsa, Italy 15
Veterans Memorial Stadium 19
Vietnam War 44
Vigorito, Joseph 99-102, 104, 112

W

Walczak, Jr., Joseph 59, 67
Ward, Frank 32
Warner Theatre 104, 109, 123, 130, 134, 147
War on Poverty 55
Washington, D.C. 25, 45, 99
Washington, George 25
Washington Magazine 99
Waytenick, Robert 120
Weber, Judge Gerald 106, 107
Welland Canal 63
Wellejus, Ed 123
"We Love Erie Days" 105
Wharton School of Finance 99
"White flight" 57
Williamson, Charles 5, 12, 13, 15, 21, 23, 27, 30-35, 38, 40, 44, 47, 52, 55, 101, 112, 126
Wilson, Woodrow 118
Worcester, Massachusetts 16
Works Progress Administration 15, 16
World War II 65, 99, 103, 129
WSEE-TV 59

Y

Yale University 6, 14
"Yankees" 9, 10, 27

(Howie Glover)

ABOUT THE AUTHOR

Originally from Illinois by way of Nevada and Georgia, Cory Vaillancourt is a freelance writer; after graduating from the University of Chicago where he focused on the history of Soviet Russia, he spent more than a decade as a political campaign consultant working for Republican and Democratic candidates across the country. Upon moving to Erie, Vaillancourt joined the Erie Reader – Erie, Pennsylvania's alternative weekly newspaper – first as a contributor, and later as a contributing editor and editor-at-large. This is his second book; compliment/heckle him at CoryVaillancourt@gmail.com.

ABOUT THE PUBLISHER

The Jefferson Educational Society of Erie (JES) is a non-profit institution founded to promote civic enlightenment and community progress for the Erie Region through the study, research, discussion, of those ideas and events that have influenced the human condition. The JES offers courses, seminars, and lectures which explain the central ideas which have formed the past, assist in exploring the present, and offer guidance to enhance the civic future of the Erie Region. For more information, visit www.jeserie.org.